# BEST OF THE RUST BELT

# BEST OF THE RUST BELT

Edited by **ANNE TRUBEK**
with an introduction by **ANNA CLARK**

Belt Publishing

First Edition 2024
ISBN: 978-1-95336-870-6

Belt Publishing
5322 Fleet Avenue, Cleveland, OH 44105
www.beltpublishing.com

Cover by David Wilson

## Selections from:

*Black in the Middle: An Anthology of the Black Midwest*
*Car Bombs to Cookie Tables: The Youngstown Anthology*
*The Chicago Neighborhood Guidebook*
*The Cincinnati Neighborhood Guidebook*
*The Cleveland Anthology*
*The Gary Anthology*
*How to Be Normal*
*The Last Children of Mill Creek*
*Midwest Architecture Journeys*
*The Milwaukee Anthology*
*The Pittsburgh Anthology*
*The Pittsburgh Neighborhood Guidebook*
*Red State Blues: Stories from Midwestern Life on the Left*
*Rust Belt Chicago*
*The St. Louis Anthology*
*Sweeter Voices Still: An LGBTQ Anthology from Middle America*
*Team Building: A Memoir about Family and the Fight for Workers' Rights*

# TABLE OF CONTENTS

Introduction by Anna Clark ...................................................1

## GROWING UP

**Traveling While Black**
*Tanisha C. Ford* ..............................................................7

**South Loop: Michigan and Harrison**
*Megan Stielstra* ............................................................12

**Notes on Summer (Or, Black Girlhood Is a Thing)**
*Britt Julious* .................................................................19

**Merluzzo**
*Sophia Benoit* ...............................................................24

**Hair**
*Lyndsey Ellis* .................................................................27

**A Girl's Youngstown**
*Jacqueline Marino* .........................................................32

**A Minute, A Pond, A North-Facing Window**
*Kim-Marie Walker* ..........................................................38

**Marquette Park: Members Only**
*Gint Aras* ....................................................................40

**Rust Belt Dreams**
*Connie Schultz* ..............................................................46

**Letter to the Prodigal Son**
*Mark Oliver* ..................................................................49

**Sunup to Sundown**
*Vivian Gibson* ......................................................................52

**How to Be Midwestern**
*Phil Christman* .....................................................................54

## CHANGING TIMES

**"The Projects":**
**Lost Public Housing Towers of the Midwest**
*Michael R. Allen* ..................................................................61

**Pilgrim on the Interstate**
*Nartana Premachandra* .........................................................67

**Long Weekend**
*Ben Gwin* .............................................................................72

**The Burgers at Miller's (Or, Dearborn's Changed)**
*Tara Rose* .............................................................................78

**Camp Dennison: A Hidden Gem Fading**
*Dani McClain* .......................................................................85

**Ruin and Porn**
*Ryan Scavnicky* .....................................................................89

**Ghosts of Bay View**
*Ken Germanson* .....................................................................95

**Something Like Irresponsibility**
*Harmony Cox* ........................................................................99

**All Sales Final**
*Sharon Bloyd-Peshkin* ..........................................................105

The Human Toll of the Steel Mill
*Joseph S. Pete* ........................................................ 112

## HUBS AND HOMES

Stay Debaucherous
*David Weathersby* ................................................ 119

The Other "Forgotten People": Feeling Blue in Missouri
*Sarah Kendzior* .................................................... 123

South Shore: Between the Lake and Emmett Till Road
*Audrey Petty* ........................................................ 128

Flea Market Urbanism
*Samantha Sanders* ............................................... 133

Photos by LaToya Ruby Frazier ........................... 140

It Is Not Waste All This,
Not Placed Here in Disgust, Street after Street
*Kathleen Rooney* ................................................. 149

What Happens at the Woodward
*Aaron Foley* ........................................................ 153

The Pennsylvania I Carry with Me
*Annie Maroon* ..................................................... 157

Flex Cleveland
*Erik Piepenburg* .................................................. 163

79
*Brian Broome* ...................................................... 168

Acknowledgments ................................................ 183
Contributors ........................................................ 185

# Introduction

## ANNA CLARK

*It is a terrible thing to be in pain and ignored—as a place, as an individual. It is perhaps worse to finally be recognized, but only as a symbol—to be given a mask and told that it's your face.*

I grew up in a small town on the Lake Michigan shore. After college in Ann Arbor, I spent a few years living in Boston. There came a point where I felt like it was time to move closer to my home-ground, and to a city that seemed like the exact opposite of Boston, which is how I came to live in Detroit.

*"Why?"* so many people asked me. Family, friends, fellow writers, and creative types: the move seemed to confuse everybody. This was 2007. I was fresh off a graduate program in fiction writing and living in a decidedly literary city. Detroit, meanwhile, faced a foreclosure crisis, a mayor under investigation, a staggering poverty rate, layoffs, buyouts, another season of excruciating losses for the Lions—just one hit after another. As usual. Detroit's story of suffering spanned generations, so familiar that it could be mistaken for normal.

*. . . to use the city incorrectly is to correct some of the city's undeniable imbalances.*

I can still hear that question—*"Why?"*—clanging with a hard edge that startled me. It sounded like: *"How could you?"*

"I have some friends there," I remember fumbling in my answer, while, weirdly, blushing. "And I just—want to?"

In years to come, my reasons would deepen. But regardless, it was plain that for many folks, choosing this haunted old city equated to giving up on my dreams. "You already escaped to the East Coast," remarked a friend in a mournful tone, as if returning to the Middle West amounted to tunneling back into prison. It's one thing to write about our lives here after we've gained a healthy distance, à la Ernest Hemingway penning stories of the North Woods in 1920s Paris, with a mitten-y map of Michigan pinned to his wall. But it's quite another thing, it seemed, to stay. If I were serious about writing, I'd be elsewhere.

To hell with that. It's such a tired take—and, still, one with maddening consequences, as Missouri writer Sarah Kendzior describes in her essay in this collection. The media executive she encountered in the wake of the 2016 presidential election had trouble believing people here have the skills to share their own stories, or that this vast swath of land has more to offer than country yarns. (Though also: who doesn't love a country yarn?)

What are you supposed to do with attitudes like this? When you are aware not only of the condescension but also how dangerous it is to ignore the lived experiences of millions and millions of people?

Challenging such willful delusion about our region is exhausting because it concedes the question. ("*Why?*") I'm mindful of writing this in an election year from a swing state that foils any fool who tries to sum it up; though, in a time of high-stakes politics, many fools try.

In 2016, Donald Trump's victory in the presidential election came with the help of states like Michigan, Wisconsin, and Pennsylvania voting red for the first time since the 1980s. Four years later, Joe Biden bested Trump in all three. This year, I have no idea what will happen. But I see old habits creep back into both the political campaigns and the media coverage. Trump attacks electric cars as a threat to our legacy industry; Biden marches with union workers and calls for the retirement of the term "Rust Belt." Pundits speculate about whether the national election will turn on federal investments in modern manufacturing and infrastructure in "key" states, or if it'll be outmatched by immigration fears. Or maybe reproductive rights. Or gas prices. Prognosticators throw up their hands: How can we know what these people are thinking? Meanwhile, states less swing-y than my own—Illinois, Indiana, Minnesota, Kentucky—are virtually erased from the public conversation.

> *Please don't give up. . . . Please try again. . . . Perhaps if I had been more courageous, you might have had an example to look up to.*

Due credit: There seems to be an emerging awareness that interviews with stray voters in Ohio diners are an insufficient mechanism for capturing the range of lived experiences here. But still, the Rust Belt is too often framed as a problem to be solved. Swinging the spotlight over to the region for fifteen minutes every time a national election rolls around, then leaving it in darkness doesn't just shortchange the people who live here; it stifles the wisdom and ingenuity that we have to offer those who live elsewhere. Making it harder to change this dynamic is the gutting of our local newsrooms, and the precariousness of jobs even at the titans of national journalism.

This is the stuff that literally keeps me up at night.

I know this: Centering more complex, more diverse stories—which is to say, truer stories—will get us to a better place. That goes for media coverage writ large as well as our individual habits of taking in news. It is more interesting, and more fun even, to turn our attention to those who take the fullness of our voices as a given and, accordingly, are building an infrastructure to amplify our most compelling stories.

In this, Belt Publishing is a pioneer. On the heels of a national recession, the press set up shop not far from Lake Erie and published anthologies about Cleveland, Detroit, and Cincinnati, each one brimming with stories and images of uncommon candor. This is how I came into the Belt family: editing the Detroit anthology. I still think of making that book as an act of listening. It takes me back to my early years in the city, and the miles and miles of watchful wandering. I reported freelance articles as an excuse to reach out to all kinds of people. It was a way to ask my new neighbors the ancient questions: "Who? What? When? Where? How? *Why*?" Here, I found a new kind of honesty in the city and in myself. By bringing me closer to what's worth writing about, Detroit made a writer out of me.

Other writers have their own stories about how their particular places unlocked something in them. Belt makes room for them: the voices that are too often overlooked, too easily simplified, too casually diminished, precisely because they are rooted in the stirring old cities, the river towns, the curious suburbs, and the rural fringe of the Rust Belt. None of this comes out of a glib sort of regional boosterism, either. Rather, it's a scaffolding for storytelling that mines complexity and vulnerability, which are at the heart of any truth.

Anthologies are still Belt's signature. It is aptly democratic. The form suits the purpose of interrogating our lives as they are lived alongside others. The Greek root of the word "anthology" is, appropriately, "a collection of flowers." A bouquet, each bloom making its neighboring blooms more beautiful.

In this one, you'll find stories collected from Belt's various books and anthologies that touch on the ghosts of Printer's Row, public housing towers, rural flea markets, the Ohio novels of Toni Morrison—there are a lot of ghosts, actually. There are also stories of reckoning with violence, trauma, displacement, addiction, grief, complicity. Changing landscapes and cityscapes. Explorations of anger. A disco poet.

Megan Stielstra distills the feeling of saying out loud for the first time, to a diner waitress named Flo in 1990s Chicago, that yes, you are a writer. There's a portrait of Detroit's storied gay bar, the Woodward, as only Aaron Foley can tell it. Phil Christman reckons with what it means to be midwestern, that nebulous region that overlaps with the Rust Belt but isn't quite the same. Brian Broome's bus ride through Pittsburgh rivals a ferry trip across the River Styx. There are histories of Wisconsin workers who fought for their rights, excavated by Ken Germanson. Intimate, interior portraits by renowned photographer LaToya Ruby Frazier. Childhood summers. Highways. Prayers. An Amish man's open letter to a kindred spirit coming up against the risk of rejection from the community for being who he really is—a risk the writer knows all too well.

There's regret. Beginnings. And far-reaching visions for our futures, plural.

To borrow a phrase from the writer and anthologist Alberto Manguel, *Best of the Rust Belt* gives us the gift of second sight, a chance to not only reread our favorites or discover what we missed but to see the flowers in a new arrangement, their shapes and colors changed.

This is the kind of book you want to recommend simply by quoting it. I indulged that impulse in this introduction, repeatedly, shamelessly out of context. But you should just read these stories yourself. Consider how they stand in conversation with one another. Notice where you find the electric shock of recognition: the feeling of seeing and being seen, sometimes when you least expect it. In all the prickly and precious ways, this book feels like home.

*—Detroit, winter 2024*

# GROWING UP

# Traveling While Black

TANISHA C. FORD

from **Black in the Middle: An Anthology of the Black Midwest**

I was somewhere between asleep and awake. It was Christmas Eve, 1987, and we were cruising up Indiana State Highway 37 in my mom's 1973 Ford Mustang—cobalt blue—making the trek from Bloomington, Indiana, to our hometown of Fort Wayne so we could celebrate Christmas with family. The sounds of Walter Hawkins's *Love Alive II*, a tape mom kept in steady rotation, were blaring through the car's speakers.

Over Hawkins's "Be Grateful," I could hear my mom in the driver's seat, bickering with my aunt, who was riding shotgun. My eight-year-old spirit registered a panic in my aunt's voice that I had never heard from her before. "Girl, we can't stop! We're in Martinsville," my aunt said.

Mom firmly told her that we had to stop because the car's headlights were out. I looked out the window, which was still slightly iced over. Darkness had chased us down, leaving nothing but a midnight blue mass of sky. In front of the Mustang, where long cylinders of white light should have been emanating to guide us up the highway, there was only black. But my aunt was willing to risk the possibility of sliding off the slick, winding road, rather than stop in Martinsville, Indiana.

I was too young to know it then, but this was the cause of the panic: We were a car of two Black women and a Black girl in a reputed sundown town of southern Indiana—after dark.

Sundown towns are communities that have historically been "all white on purpose," their whiteness enforced either officially (in the past, some towns had signs posted with messages like "Whites Only Within City Limits After Dark") or through unofficial, often violent means. Thousands of sundown towns existed across the country. By some estimates, there were as many as two hundred in Indiana alone. And they are not unique to small towns—James Loewen, in his book *Sundown Towns: A Hidden Dimension of American Racism*, identifies "sundown suburbs" of larger cities. Many sundown towns remain overwhelmingly, if not exclusively, white.

News of Black folks being threatened, beaten, and lynched in places like these spread rapidly through our communities' informal networks. Some of those stories had been circulating since the 1920s and 1930s, when there was a resurgence in Klan activity in Indiana and across the US. Black women were particularly vulnerable to beatings and lynchings, as well as sexual assaults. It's what prompted the publication of *The Negro Motorists' Green Book* in 1936 (which was published regularly until 1966). The only people who have the luxury of ignoring this history are those who haven't had to order their lives by that unofficial rule and the vigilante violence that was promised if you were caught in a sundown town at dusk.

Beyond its reputation as a sundown town, Martinsville was also known as the epicenter of Klan terror in Indiana. I had never heard of Martinsville before, but I was intrigued by this infamous place that could reduce a grown woman to near tears. I jolted up in my seat, butting into the conversation. "What's Martinsville? What's wrong with the car? What are you scared of, Aunt Janice? Are we gonna make it home in time to open my Christmas gifts?"

No one in our car uttered the words "sundown town"; that was a language I'd come to know later in life. For now, I was getting a particular kind of geography lesson. I didn't know where Martinsville was on a map in relationship to Fort Wayne, but I was learning that I wasn't supposed to be there. I added it to a list that included Waynedale and Huntington, places I'd also heard the adults in my life say to stay clear of. Conversely, in Indianapolis, we could find communities of people who looked like us, soul food restaurants, concerts, and big events like the Circle City Classic, which catered to Black folks.

The lesson was clear: navigating the state was less about knowing direction and more about knowing "your place." Mom and Aunt Janice seemed to know—instinctively, it seemed—where they belonged and where they didn't. And clearly, Martinsville was the latter.

―――――――

We pulled into a mom-and-pop gas station. A string of Christmas lights framed the shop window. The clerk on duty, an older white man, peeked his head out. Seeing our dark bodies emerging from the car, he walked outside slowly with a perplexed look on his face. Presumably, because Black folks knew to steer clear of Martinsville, whites in Martinsville had become accustomed to rarely, if ever, seeing us in real life.

My mother explained what had brought us to his establishment on this crisp winter evening. I searched the man's eyes for some telltale sign of his comfort level. He wasn't outwardly hostile—I'd experienced overt racism enough times in my young life to know what it looked like. But he also wasn't kind in that way that Mom and Dad's white friends who came to the house were.

Mom and the clerk performed an awkward dance of human politeness as he led us into the gas station so Mom could call my father collect. He offered us space to sit inside while we waited for my father to arrive. Aunt Janice was fixing her mouth to say "hell no!" when my mother jumped in and politely declined his offer, saying we would wait in the car. Mom and Aunt Janice poured cups of the shop's bitter coffee to help them stay alert. We made our way back to the car.

No one bothered us. Not even the clerk, who had returned to his mundane shop duties. But my mother and aunt began sharing stories with me—some joyous, some utterly terrifying—about what it was like to be college students in Klan country during the peak years of the Black Power Movement.

In 1968, just four years before my mother arrived on IU's campus, a twenty-one-year-old Black encyclopedia saleswoman named Carol Jenkins was brutally murdered in Martinsville by a Klan member. The murder went unsolved for more than three decades. Meanwhile, hundreds of young Black women like my mother left their homes each year to attend IU, the specter of Jenkins's murder a constant reminder that they could never—and would never—feel or be safe.

The racial violence of the area was even more explicit for my family. My mom told me her brother, my Uncle Howard, was beaten bloody in Martinsville when he, not being from the area, stopped to get food on his way to visit her at college.

The IU campus wasn't even a refuge from anti-Black harassment. My mom told stories of the KKK marching on public streets. University police officers would harass Black students for gathering on the yard in groups considered "too large." White professors assumed that Black students were not prepared for the rigors of college, often grading them more harshly than their white counterparts. Many of these stories of racial discrimination on campus were chronicled in the IU Arbutus yearbook, given titles such as "Black Life in the Ivory Tower." These stories mirrored those written on the pages of *Essence* in the early seventies, by and about Black students at predominantly white institutions.

Up until that Christmas Eve, the only depictions I'd seen of the Klan were in films, like the scene in *Lady Sings the Blues* (1972), in which Klan members attack Billie Holiday's tour bus, hitting her in the eye with the butt of a wooden stake. But here I was now, hearing of my own family's encounters with these enigmas in white hoods. I now understood that there were fleshy bodies underneath those hoods—real people—who hated us simply because we were Black.

--------

But in the quiet spaces of their dorm rooms and apartments, Mom and her peers could dance out their rage, they could style out their rage. I could hear it in their voices, in the ways they told their stories, but it would not truly sink in until I was much older: survival then—as it is now—was about stealing moments of intoxicating pleasure amidst many more that were singed by violence.

I heard tales of Black, sweaty bodies doing dances like the Dawg and the Hustle at the annual Omega Psi Phi Mardi Gras Party. Mom and her friends would go decked out in elephant-leg pants—bout the widest bell-bottoms you'll ever see—and lace-front dresses and knee-high boots, with their Afros picked just so. Those parties were safe havens where young Black folks, who were few in number on campus, could dance and listen to soul and funk tracks—unapologetically young and Black.

My mom and my aunt had gotten into a rhythm, telling their stories, feeding off of each other like a well-trained performance duo. Black girl hand gestures abounded. Aunt Janice would let out her signature screeching cackle when things got really funny. Mom's voice would boom when she told one of her "bet not no one mess with me" stories. They laughed as they tried to remember the name of "so-and-so's boyfriend" who did "woopty woop" at "such-and-such's" apartment "that one night." I learned of the men my mom loved long before she and my father became a thing.

I would interject here and there with questions, wanting more details to add to the mental movie of the past that I was directing in my head. But for the most part, I knew to keep quiet because something big, something important was happening here. This was more than a mere passing of the time. This was two Black women trying to work through fear and trauma, sharing their vulnerability with me, a girl of a different era, of a different generation, but of the same blood. Through them, I experienced the full range of Black emotion, their stories offering a context for my aunt's fear earlier that evening. It came from a real place.

By the time my father dashed up to the gas station in his big, mint green Mercury Cougar to rescue his wife and daughter, I felt a little older, a little less innocent. I had come face-to-face with white supremacy, learning at a young age that people will do anything—including taking a life— in order to maintain some semblance of power. It was a rite of passage that, even then, I knew my white peers did not have to experience. Their privilege shielded them from ever having to learn about this real American horror story. Yet, the trauma of the past was now etched into my skin. To be a Black girl in this world meant pain would be part of the experience.

But my passage also taught me about Black resilience, Black joy, Black creativity. Something about sharing the tiny space of the old Mustang with my mom and my aunt helped us to bond. For those few hours, we were on equal footing. All of us scared, and them telling stories to keep the haints away. The stories were our survival. The air never went silent.

# South Loop:
# Michigan and Harrison

MEGAN STIELSTRA

from **The Chicago Neighborhood Guidebook**

## 1995

I'm at the Harrison, a diner in the South Loop on Harrison Street between Michigan Avenue and Wabash. This place has vinyl booths. It has bottomless coffee for a buck twenty-five. The waitresses are in their fifties; they smoke and wear orthopedic shoes, and if you're rude or tip like crap, they give you a look. *Think about how you treat people*, it says. *Think about the kind of person you want to be*. One of them calls me "Honey." She has bleached hair high with Aquanet, and she's chewing hot pink bubble gum. In my memory her name is Flo, but I was twenty then, and I'm forty now, and when I was six, I watched that show *Alice* with my babysitter, so it's possible I'm thinking of Polly Holliday.

"Here you go, Honey," she says, refilling my coffee. I like it when she calls me that. Makes me feel like I'm her girl, like she's watching out for me. Lord knows I need it. I pour in sugar, a faucet-like stream from the dispenser. When I think of myself then, alone in a new city with all my desperate dreams, the first thing I remember is coffee, thick and heavy, too-too sweet. I remember the backs of my thighs sticking to the booths. I remember Flo looking at the stack of books in front of me and asking, "You a writer?"

"Yes," I say.

It's the first time I said it out loud. The first time I believed it.

I came to Chicago for college, my third in three states in three years. I studied journalism and hated it, then English literature, which was better but still not me. I wanted to write stories, but you can't go to school for that, right? Where I was from in small-town Michigan, you majored in education or agriculture or nursing—steady salary and 401(k). Still, when my sophomore-year boyfriend* said he wanted to move to Chicago, I went to an internet café and punched "creative" and "writing" into Yahoo. An art school came up in the South Loop, the corner of Michigan and Harrison. Its fiction program was housed in the School of Performing Arts, which seemed so totally radical, a place that treated writing like theater or painting or music. I applied, got a transfer scholarship, and showed up for orientation in the blistering sauna of summertime Chicago.

I remember coming up from the underground at the Red Line stop at Harrison: asphalt, sidewalk, brick. Tangible humidity, a baking blanket spread over the grid. Straight north was the Chicago Public Library, with its massive red walls and sculptures looking down from the roof—owls, I'd later learn, for knowledge. I walked east between parking lots and graffiti and iron fire escapes hanging precariously off the sides of buildings eight, nine, ten stories high toward a vertical slice of open sky: Michigan Avenue, Grant Park, the lake. I passed kids smoking on the sidewalk, kids with tattoos and books and cameras. They were women and men and both and neither, old and young and *how can you tell?* Later, in class, I'd learn about their lives: Vietnam vets and single mothers and recent immigrants and dumb, scared kids like me. We were, most all of us, broke. We had two or three jobs. We worked hard and partied hard—some of us harder than we should have—and we crashed and burned and got back up, but above all else, we made things.

It was my place.

I was there for twenty years.

It's different now, of course. They gutted the Harrison. There's a fast-food-style counter in its place; Styrofoam cups, get it 'n go. I'd pass it on the way to my office and watch the college students through the windows.

# 2000

I'm at George's, a rat trap of a dive bar on the corner of Wabash and Balbo. It butts up to a parking lot. It's open 'til 4:00 a.m. It's small—Five tables? Six? Five or six stools at the bar?—and felt exactly like sitting on the inside of an ashtray. This was years before the Smoke Free Illinois Act banned smoking in public buildings. I didn't smoke, but five minutes in George's was a full-on contact high. You could feel the smoke in your pores, taste

---

* I don't know what happened to that guy.

it in the baskets of popcorn from the free machine in the back, smell it in your hair and clothes and nails for days.

How else to say it?—this place is *perfect*.

I come here after class to shut down my brain. I'd line up my quarters and play "Barracuda" on the jukebox until the bartender promised me shots if I stopped. When I think of myself back then, working days in a brunch restaurant, taking three night classes a week toward my MFA plus student teaching, the first thing I remember is bourbon—with coke, with ice, with nothing. I remember the dull, fuzzy buzz and no sleep. I remember sitting at the bar and talking about books. Everything was books. I could tell you about Lorian, Ohio, where Pecola lived in *The Bluest Eye*. The Isle of Sky in *To the Lighthouse*. Sunset Park in *Last Exit to Brooklyn*. Macondo and Robledo and Asgard and Lothlorien—places that live only in our heads.

"But what do you know about here?" asks the bartender. He's an older guy, his accent thick. He opens his arms like he's showing me the world. Or maybe he's showing me the city. Or maybe Congress to Cermack, Lake Shore Drive to the Chicago River, this neighborhood I come to every day and don't know shit about.

What do you know about the place where you live? Where you work, go to school, where your kids go to school?

The next morning, I went to the library and read about the South Loop: its history as the country's railway epicenter, the Midwest's largest printing district, its experiments in urban planning. It housed waves of European immigrants, shipping magnates in their mansions, and Chicago's version of a vice district, brothels both drug-addled and couture. I read about the Fort Dearborn Massacre during the War of 1812. I read about Pacific Garden, the "oldest, continuously operating rescue mission in the country." I read about gentrification and the part I played in it, the beginning of an ongoing conversation I have with myself about what it means to contribute ethically to a community, a city, the world.

In a recent interview, I was asked to name the most important thing I learned in graduate school.

I thought of that night at George's.

They tore the place down in early 2016 to make room for high-rise apartments, which, according to the developer, feature "amenities and floor plans tailored to the needs of today's Millennial renter." He declined to say how much they would cost.

Do me a favor. If you're ever near the corner of Wabash and Balbo, give a little whisper: "Hey, George."

It's not a place that history will remember. The least we can do is wave.

# 2005

I'm at Gourmand, a coffee shop on Dearborn just north of Polk. It has mismatched couches from thrift stores. It has open mic poetry readings. It has giant chalkboards with the day's specials, weird* local art, and weird local artists writing and drawing and meeting and scheming. I like the energy, the accountability. If all these people are working, then I have to work, too. I get coffee and camp out in a ratty velvet chair, reading student writing. I have adjunct gigs at colleges in the South Loop and Hyde Park, and I teach writing and performance in community organizations around the city. When I think of myself then, running from classrooms to libraries to living rooms, the first thing I remember are folders of stories, people putting their hearts on a page and handing those pages to me. I read about growing up young in Chicago, female in Chicago, Black in Chicago, queer in Chicago—the joy and the fear and the fight. Everything I do has been influenced by those stories; how I write, teach, parent, vote.

Thank you for trusting me.

"Megan?"

It's a student, here for a meeting. She'd asked if we could talk in my office and was surprised when I said I didn't have one. I get it. When I was in her shoes, I didn't know that some of my professors didn't have an office or, for that matter, a salary. I didn't know that 48 percent of college teachers in this country were part-time; no benefits, no job security. I didn't think about how that would affect my education. She sits on the ratty velvet loveseat and we talk about what she's reading. We talk about what she's writing. We talk about what she's scared of writing—it's too personal, her parents can't know, if he finds out he'll get mad, no she doesn't want to go to the police, she's having nightmares, panic attacks, can't breathe.

This is not the first time a young person has come to me about sexual assault. It is not the last.

---

* I like weird.

The specifics of our conversation are not mine to tell, but it ends with her asking if I'll go with her to the college's counseling office. We bus our table, pack our stuff, pile into sweaters and scarves. "Can we talk about something else?" she asks as we walk. "Please? I don't care what, I just don't want to think about it for a minute." I start saying whatever comes into my head because it's a thing she asked of me that I can do, even though what I want to do is cry. I point up at the twelve-story clock tower at Dearborn Station and tell her how I first read about it in *The Jungle* by Upton Sinclair. I tell her how they block off these streets every year for the Printer's Row Lit Festival and someday she can be part of it. I tell her how in the late 1800s, the buildings surrounding us housed printing presses and linotype manufacturers, the foremothers of the books we read today, a century of back-and-forth between reader and writer. I tell her that when they built the University Center super-dorm the year before, they had to reroute the entire Brown Line and I'd stand beneath the broken tracks scared the "L" would fall. I tell her about a bar called George's where I drank during grad school. I tell her about a diner called the Harrison, a waitress called Flo. I tell her I'll sit with her until her triage appointment and that if they can't give her one today, I will burn the building to the fucking ground.

"I know," she says, smiling. "That's why I asked you to come."

So much has changed. Gourmand is a bike shop. 76.4 percent of college professors are adjunct. The University Center sold to a developer for 200 mil.

But god. So much is still the same.

## 2010

I'm at Cafecito, a blink-and-you'll-miss-it Cuban place on Congress. I don't want to give this place away—the line is already too long, out the door and onto the street. It has ropa vieja. It has caldo gallego. It has the best café con leche I've had in my life. My coffee intake is forever on the rise. I have a full-time job at the college in faculty development ("Can we meet for coffee?"), a night class at a different college (student conferences in coffee shops), a two-year-old child (omg coffee), a bitch of a thyroid disorder, the primary symptom of which is fatigue (hence coffee), a two-hour daily commute (coffee to go!), little to no sleep (duh), and this, my friends, is the American Dream.

The truth?—I love it.

"Where have you been?" says the man ahead of me in line. I work with hundreds of teachers; it's not possible for me to remember everyone's name, but I remember that I like him à la Maya Angelou: *People will forget what you said, people will forget what you did, but people will never forget how you made them feel.* I know he teaches in the journalism department. This was back before journalism merged with, I think, marketing? There have been a lot of merges.

"Took some time off," I tell him, leaving out specifics: the postpartum depression, the mess in my head, the ongoing work of healing and how happy I am to be back in the world. My tiny son is healthy now, thriving. I'm writing again. Every day I talk to teachers trying to change things for the better and about how lucky we are to do work that means something in this beautiful mess of a life.

"Well," he says. "Welcome back!" and I feel like singing. I feel blood in my veins. I feel a little bonkers, but who the hell cares? I get my café and head east up Congress, the long way around to my office. The sun climbs over the lake. People everywhere with their coffee and their stories, waiting for the bus, rushing to work, walking lazily through the park at 8:00 a.m. on Wednesday. A thousand cars zip by, speeding and furious to Lake Shore Drive North and 290 West and South on 94, and here I am in the middle of everything, alive, alive, alive.

# 2015

I'm at the Starbucks at Michigan and Balbo, just below the lobby of the Blackstone Hotel. You've been to this place, or one exactly like it: long line. Crowd waiting at the back counter. Separate station for cream and sugar; the chalky, grating sound of the steamer; little to no seating. This location doesn't let you sit with a laptop or a friend, no endless conversations about books, just get your caffeine and GTFO. It serves the whole South Loop, as well as tourists in Grant Park and the entire college community, literally thousands of students and faculty looking for a jump-start after all-nighters writing papers or reading papers or grading papers—*writereadgrade writereadgrade* in a never-ending ouroboros loop.

"Hey, honey," says Kathy, and puts in my order. She knows what I like. She has a photographic memory for all our stupid, frothy adjectives: *nonfat no-whip double-shot with room.* I don't let anyone call me "Honey," but from her, it's lovely. Like she's looking out for me.

Lord knows.

I come here every day, sometimes twice. She makes my drink and we talk about our kids. It's nice to talk about something other than what's happening at the college: programs cut, scholarships gutted, faculty fired or jumping ship.

*Think about the kind of person you want to be.*

"Shit. You, too?" Kathy says, nodding at my backpack, an enormous outdoor sport model that you'd take up a mountain for a month, plus several paper-packed tote bags hanging at my sides. I'd just cleared out my cubicle. My file cabinet. My bookshelf. My back hurts. My head, my heart.

"I'm sorry," she says. I know she means it.

"It's okay," I say, and I mean that, too.

I walk out onto Michigan Avenue; the summer, the sauna. I turn the corner at Harrison; asphalt, sidewalk, brick. There are condos. Townhouses. Specialty grocery stores and commissioned murals and tourists. The neighborhood—the city—is so different from when I first arrived. I'm trying to remember myself back then. I had an apartment in Ukranian Village. Later, I moved to Wicker Park, then Logan Square, then four years in four apartments in Humboldt Park. Five years in Uptown. Six in Rogers Park. I waited tables in Little Italy, River North, and Bucktown; a decade at the Bongo Room on Milwaukee Avenue; teaching in Hyde Park, Oak Park, Ravenswood, Evanston, Cabrini Green, the Gold Coast, the Loop—I can't remember everywhere anymore. What I do know is this: in my twenty years of trying to get by and make things in this beautiful, complicated city, the only place that was ever constant was that corner of Michigan and Harrison.

It's not my place anymore.

Doesn't mean it was easy to leave.

On the way to my car, I pass the food counter where the Harrison used to be and watch the college students through the windows. Their desperate dreams, their tables stacked with books. Jesus, they put a lot of sugar in their coffee.

# Notes on Summer (Or, Black Girlhood Is a Thing)

## BRITT JULIOUS

from **Rust Belt Chicago**

## I.

Summer is fleeting and so am I. The me of a good summer is as temporary as the leaves on the trees, the thick viscosity that glides across our limbs we call "humid air." It is as temporary as a gelato cone, the remnants of which I'll lick off my fingers and down my hand and even across the tattoo on my arm sometime later today and tomorrow and for the rest of the days when the heat feels equally brutal and rejuvenating.

When the me of a good summer arrives, I try best not to acknowledge it. To see the fulfillment of hot days and cold drinks pouring down my throat is like spotting an animal in the wild. This momentary thing is lovely and great until it is gone. In reality, I am trying to recapture the me of my youth.

## II.

I say I grew up in two places, and that is somewhat true. Oak Park, a suburb of Chicago, is where I spent the majority of my time. We first lived in an apartment before purchasing our own home on the southwest side of the town. But, maybe through the lens of nostalgia, I recognize Austin as my home too.

My grandparents live in the Austin neighborhood in a beautiful and traditional American foursquare house. There, the sidewalks are wide and easy to maneuver. Sometimes I pounce across the concrete of my current hood, crimping my limbs against storefronts and light poles so as not to take up space as others—young mothers with rowdy children and strollers, packs of girlfriends out for a night on the town, aggressive young men looking not for a hand but a pair of breasts and an ass to grab—pass me by.

But in Austin, I remember how wide the block seemed. Sometimes I sat down on the sidewalk, and from my line of vision, the houses reached far beyond where the eye could see. Even now, when I visit as an adult, I can see the history there. When we moved to Oak Park, my sister and I tried to play outdoors, but we largely played inside. This was different than in Austin, where the freedom and joy of girlhood played out on sidewalks and in backyards.

When I say there is history there, I mean there is a history of childhood, of innocence, of the power of play. Our Oak Park block was quiet, but in Austin there was there there. There was the energy born out of time enjoyed. It was something I didn't know I needed until it was not there.

Strongest in my memory is a young girl named Nicole. She lived down the street from my grandmother. She had long, dark, curly hair and a pinched face that I thought was lovely at the time but makes me wince now. I'm not sure why.

She was older than me but didn't seem that way. I followed my older sister Kourtney around like a shadow and Nicole in turn did that to me. A part of me was secretly thrilled by this. No longer was I reliant on the whims of someone else. Instead, my ideas of fun, my actions, my words held precedence in the mind of another person. I was a leader who knew it but never got the chance to show it. It was not lost on me too that her name was my sister's middle name. There was a lineage in our girlhood, from the second name of my kin to the first name of my friend.

We played together in summertime, mostly. I was out of school, and my parents needed our time to be spent. I remember this not because of the weather but the amount of play. School is a blur, but summers stand firm in my mind. Play happened when the sun was heaviest. Friendships formed heaviest during this time too.

She followed me around to the corner store, where we purchased cheap candies. She followed me a half a block down to the woman who sold sno-cones from her front porch. She followed me as I got into inappropriate arguments with my grandparents' next-door neighbor, Mr. Underwood, about things he said that I found dumb. She followed me even as we ran up and down the block. I was a chubby kid, so I think she slowed down to follow me when we did that in particular.

I don't know when we met, but it's difficult to discern most things from one's early childhood. The way memories form during that time is that suddenly, something or someone is a part of your life and that is that. So, suddenly, Nicole was a part of my life. Suddenly, she was there and I didn't question it.

Right now, I am thinking about my grandparents' large backyard. There is a rose bush square in the middle, surrounded by lush grass. My grandparents would inflate a kiddie pool and fill it with cold water running through a hose and we'd jump around and play. Nicole never really said much. Instead, she let me do the talking, and talk I did: about how I knew mosquitos had it out for us, about how much better orange slices were than chocolate, about why my grandmother made the best macaroni and cheese in the world and no one could say differently to me.

Most importantly though, Nicole was an actual friend. She was there and she listened and she didn't question one's intentions. She was present. She laughed harder than anyone I knew and stomped her feet when she was stressed. She was human and viable.

"I hate when you are not here," she used to say, and I felt the same way.

When you are a child, you need people like that in your life, and when you are an adult, or even just on the cusp of becoming one, you realize how difficult it is to find that in others. Suddenly, the realities of the world strike hard and fast and don't let go. Suddenly, there are responsibilities and sadness and men, hovering over your mind and your limbs, eager to take and take and take until they don't need you anymore. If you find a friend like that and you are not seven, you must hold on to them as much and for as long as possible. The world doesn't spin for young women with sturdy ground to walk on and grow.

The more my family settled into our life in our house in Oak Park, the less the Austin neighborhood felt like a home. It was a quick, five-minute drive to my grandparents' house, but even that seemed too far away. Houses create homes, and homes create new narratives. My family was building a new narrative for ourselves. There was a fork in the road, and we took a different path, one that allowed us to fulfill lifelong dreams but also separated us, however slowly, from the things we once knew.

"You know, Nicole always asks about you," my grandmother would say to me when I visited as I got older.

"So?" I would respond.

"Don't you want to say hi?" she asked me.

"Why would I do that?" I would respond and then curl up on the couch with my heavy head placed solidly on my grandmother's lap. I was there to visit my family. I was not there to see other people. My grandparents' home, and in turn, the Austin neighborhood, became a place I went to and not a place I came from. It was not me anymore.

But I did see her one day. My grandmother was particularly convincing, and so I walked down the street, but I couldn't remember where she lived. The houses hadn't changed, but they all blended in with each other at that point. An American foursquare was an American foursquare was an American foursquare. The only thing I recognized on that block was my grandparents' home, shining like a light against the blurred structures surrounding it.

There were people on the porch of one home, an older woman and a young man, and they looked at me as if they knew me, and not from a pleasant experience. They looked hard and long, and I tried to keep their gaze until I looked down, exhausted by the weight of their stares. I walked back, and when my grandmother asked if I said hello, I said yes. She never truly asked me about it again.

I am not sure when girlhood is lost, but I am sure of all of the ways I tried to recapture it. I began to dance as a young girl, and the more I danced, the more in control I felt. These are my legs that bend and curve, my arms that flex. Freedom stemmed from the control I gained, and to dance was to be free. I didn't recognize it then, but I pushed through the grueling rehearsals with the knowledge that once I learned a routine, it would become something I could call on at a moment's notice. At any moment after, I could become this powerful being in control of my movements and myself, unhurried or torn apart. My movements were choreographed and not choreographed. When I had a moment to move about the floor on my own terms, that is when I felt most alive. It was a moment without judgment, just sadness and anxiety and excitement manifest through a pirouette, a switch leap, a flick of the wrist. As I got older, I leaned in to this activity. Each performance was a temporary girlhood high, a me reclaimed, a sense of self and empowerment found.

Black girlhood is summer. It arrives quick and dies just as fast. Suddenly we are young women, even if we don't feel it, even if we know intrinsically there is life left to live. In childhood, we are given the freedom to firmly be ourselves. There is nothing too high or too far or too great for us. No, instead, everything is within reach. It's not just innocence. It is, I think, a true sense of self. It is ourselves at our most actualized. As adults, we will do whatever is necessary to recapture that feeling. I still feel it now, that desire to recapture the me of my girlhood. It is also why our friendships feel truer in that time than maybe any other time in our lives. Unburdened by the weight of the world, we are free to be ourselves.

That is why summer feels so precious and why Chicago summers especially feel so critical. When people say Chicago summers are better than anywhere else, they are not lying. I feel that deeply in my bones. It is Chicago summers that shaped me, made me confident, made me into a strong and capable woman before I ever really knew it.

# Merluzzo

## SOPHIA BENOIT

from **The St. Louis Anthology**

My father has been trying—mostly with terrible results—to entice me to come back to St. Louis for seven years. Well, the first year after I left for school in the "lost, anchorless, soulless" city of Los Angeles (his words), he didn't have to do much. I had a boyfriend back in St. Louis and was coming back often anyway. After that ended, however, the price of flights somehow felt every penny of their $350. First it was staying in LA for its mild summers, where not a single person decries that it's "not the heat, it's the humidity." Eventually, I worked my way up to missing Thanksgiving, something that has left me wracked with guilt (although most things do, so it's not a great barometer).

Once my father caught on to the fact that my trips were going to become less and less frequent—though still about three times a year, which is pretty great if I do say so myself—and that my life in Los Angeles was becoming permanent, he had to get more creative with the enticements. First, it was mostly shooting related: "We can do target practice in the garage if Katy isn't home" (This piece may be how my stepmother finds out about that). "Do your friends in California have guns?" (They do not).

Anything that seemed antithetical to the Missourian image of what California stands for was fodder for him. We're having pork steaks; come home. We got illegal fireworks; you should come home. There's a family of foxes living under the porch and I'm feeding them rotisserie chickens from Schnucks; come back before they leave. Once, I came home to find him building a makeshift trampoline under our front porch light because a nest of baby birds was going to learn to fly soon and he had really taken to them. God knows how the other baby birds of the world make it without the careful attention of my father.

Eventually, he changed tactics: food. It's a smart move, since he's a great cook and I'm an even better eater. This isn't typical St. Louis food, however. He doesn't try to get me to come home with promises of concretes or toasted ravioli. There isn't Provel cheese on the table.

Sometimes it's something as simple as him wanting to try out the pressure cooker, which never really seems to work properly; the risk of explosion is half the fun. Recently, he wanted to try out a new sausage shop. It's easy to lure me back in winter months, since every New Year, we make *bagna cauda*, a dish of melted butter, oil, garlic, salt, and anchovies that you then dip vegetables and bread into. Despite the name, which means "hot bath" in Italian, the dish itself is a revelation, as most things made of melted butter are. We also often make jars of homemade pesto to give out as Christmas gifts.

Don't steal this idea, but homemade pesto is an amazing gift. Store-bought pesto will quickly disappoint after you've made it fresh. I know that sounds like something Ina Garten would say, but it's the truth. When I was younger, each of us five kids had a specific job when it came to making pesto, whether it was grating cheese, chopping nuts, or mine, which was to carefully cut the basil plant leaves. Recently, I was home for one of my father's quarterly trips to Viviano's. I'm not even sure that they sell anything he couldn't find elsewhere, but I think being in a shop full of Italian food makes him feel at home. As usual, my father got salted cod. It took twenty-five years of trying to wear me down before this time, mostly out of guilt that I'm not home enough, I agreed to "try" it. I don't particularly like fish, but he told me the story of his Nonna making *merluzzo*, the Italian word for cod but also the general name they used for a dish of cod, onions, and polenta. Polenta was really the selling point for me. There's almost nothing you can make out of cornmeal I won't eat.

My grandfather came from a town outside of Turin called Salto, which means "to leap." An appropriately named place to leave, I suppose. Upon visiting the town, however, any modern American would wonder at leaving; it's overwhelmingly beautiful. Nestled in the verdant foothills of (the also appropriately named) Piedmont, my family that is still there lives on a small, mostly defunct vineyard from the early 1800s, surrounded by a not-at-all-defunct fruit orchard. They're a family of butchers, a job that seems to be from another time, and which only adds to the charm of visiting.

When my grandfather left, however, the area was struggling; his father left first and stayed in America for seven years, going through Ellis Island before arriving in the Italian enclave of Collinsville, Illinois. There, he established a blacksmith shop and eventually sent for his wife and two sons. When my grandfather arrived, the story goes, he was placed in school a few years lower than his actual age, mostly because he didn't speak any English. This strategy seems a bit odd to me: why would fourth-grade English be any easier than sixth-grade English? Perhaps out of the frustration at this process, he vowed that once he learned English, he would not speak Italian again. This is how my family lost the language, a source of an odd amount of grief for some of us. When you tell someone that your father is Italian or that your grandfather is, one of the first questions is, "So, do you speak Italian?" Plus, there's nothing more magical to monolingual Americans than little babies and children who can seamlessly slip between two languages. We were robbed of that, but the food stayed.

For as much as my grandfather tried to divorce himself from the language, he still competed in Bocce tournaments and became a butcher, just like his family back home. And his children all learned to grow basil for homemade pesto, and "flip" the pot of polenta, letting it spill onto the counter to harden, and melt anchovies for *banga cauda*.

That's because you don't lose your home when you leave; you carry small, surprising pieces of it with you. When I came to Los Angeles— admittedly, a much shorter cultural jump than moving from Italy—I brought some of St. Louis. I still wave "thank you" at other drivers if they let me in. I refuse to call anything a "freeway." I feed people every time they come to my house. I have mastered a gooey butter cake recipe. I was the only person in my friend group who knew that the animal we encountered in the bushes on campus was just a possum. I prefer thin crust pizza, although I'm not sure you can say that's a St. Louis thing. I'm still better than average at cornhole. I love a good trip to Target. In many ways, I am distinctly midwestern.

Someday, I might have to get my own children to come back to me. I won't use cod. I'll probably stick with gooey butter cake.

# Hair

## LYNDSEY ELLIS

### from **Black in the Middle: An Anthology of the Black Midwest**

In the summer of 2001, I chose to go natural for the first time. The decision, I thought, had more to do with preserving the hair I had left than making a political statement. Excessive heat from curling irons, on top of years of relaxers, had caused my ends to thin, and I wanted to do something about it before starting my freshman year in college.

Cheryl, my best friend, was also entering University of Missouri-Columbia, which was two hours outside of our hometown. She liked the idea of going natural and wanted to do it with me. We made a bet that whoever didn't last and returned to the perm first would pay the other's cell phone bill for the remainder of the school year.

I was glad I wasn't alone, but I knew Cheryl had it easier. She had fine hair that frizzed in the heat but didn't nap up like the thick tufts covering my scalp. All she had to do was smooth down her sides with a damp brush and pull the rest into a ponytail at the crown of her head.

Me? I had to get radically creative. At the time, I was afraid of dreadlocks, or the idea of trying to maintain them. The only folks I knew who could pull it off were celebrities I'd seen in magazines or in music videos on television, like Lauryn Hill, Res, Lenny Kravitz, and Whoopi. I didn't know anyone personally who wore them except Cheryl's mother, Ms. Pam. But like Cheryl, her mother was on the verge of having what was called "good" hair. Even when we saw Ms. Pam at her worst, looking exhausted after working another graveyard shift, her edges were always laid.

Knowing my experience would be drastically different, I went with letting my new growth accumulate the entire summer until I had a tiny afro and cut off my thinning ends. Then, before the semester started, I got braids because I couldn't bear getting used to short hair in public.

Cheryl and I lived in separate dorms, but we were together all the time. We had the same mutual friends. We went to the same parties. We did the same drugs. We talked shit about the same people. We even had a course together: Literature of the African Diaspora. A small class with more women than men, and an almost equal mix of Blacks and whites, which was a rarity at our ultrawhite university.

Dr. O, our professor, was a Nigerian man. Tall and lean, with a strong jawline and chestnut brown skin. Dr. O's class exposed us to various Black poets and writers around the world whose works focused on Black expression and race relations. For the first time, I read *Things Fall Apart* by Chinua Achebe, *Sonny's Blues* by James Baldwin, "Recitatif " by Toni Morrison, and several other classic works. Ultimately, that's when I discovered that I too wanted to be a creative writer, although I wasn't ready to have that conversation outside of my head yet.

Cheryl and I—both closemouthed and self-conscious when we weren't partying on nights and weekends—were two of the only three Black women in the class. The other one, Jade, was a lanky, outspoken fair-skinned woman with natural cropped hair who sat in the front center row. Cheryl and I mocked Jade outside of class; we thought she looked like she reeked of incense, read tarot cards as a side hustle, and got dressed in the dark with hand-me-downs from the local Goodwill.

But Jade knew a lot of history, especially controversial history with dark secrets revealing the depth of racism that shaped the Midwest. A college junior, she'd worked as a campus tour guide for incoming freshmen the previous summer, and she wasn't shy about pointing out local atrocities she'd discovered to our class. One instance, she said, involved Lloyd L. Gaines, a man who'd drawn attention after being denied admission to the University of Missouri-Columbia's law school because he was Black. Gaines's family had been part of the Great Migration and settled in St. Louis from rural Mississippi in the 1920s. There, Gaines flourished academically and later attended Lincoln University, a historically Black college in Jefferson City, Missouri. After graduating, he applied to law school and filed suit when he was rejected. The US Supreme Court ruled in Gaines's favor, but while waiting on classes to open, he traveled to Chicago, where he disappeared, never to be heard from again.

In 2000, Mizzou's Black Culture Center was named after Gaines to keep his legacy alive. While one of the unproved theories is that Gaines gave up and relocated to Mexico, legend has it that he was murdered by angry white supremacists who buried his bones somewhere on the university's grounds. I remember hearing several accounts from students who claimed they saw Gaines's ghost roaming around campus.

In Dr. O's class, there was also a rambunctious brother we called Wu-Tang. Thick-necked and bowlegged, he was a hip-hop head whose headphones complemented the hoodies he donned over his football jersey, and his box braids always looked fresh. Wu-Tang wasn't your everyday jock, though. His conversation was smooth and intelligent. He loved reading, and it showed in his analyses of our reading assignments during class discussions. Many times, from his seat in the back of the room, Wu-Tang would refute or echo Jade's responses to Dr. O's questions. The two of them would publicly face off until the discussion morphed into a semi-heated debate, but by the end of class, they'd be laughing and cracking jokes on each other like it was all for sport.

"Bet you they're fucking," Cheryl said to me one day after class.

"Nah," I told her, "they don't seem like each other's type."

"Them be the ones."

"Girl, whatever."

I waved off her assumption. Wu-Tang, I thought, was more inclined to mess around with one of the sorority chicks like Alison, who sat catercorner to Cheryl and me. Alison, or Cool White Girl as we called her, looked like most of the other white girls on campus with her blonde highlights, eye makeup, and flip-flops, but she seemed friendlier without being fake nice. She greeted us in class and even when we crossed paths on campus. She also wasn't afraid to challenge Jade or Wu-Tang in a class discussion.

One day, Dr. O. asked the class to think of a time when someone around us gave life to a misconception about a different race or culture. It seemed like a packed question that would lead to many interesting answers by those crazy enough to respond. Gradually, people spit out their answers. Alison raised her hand. When Dr. O. called on her, she opened her mouth but nothing came out. Her hands, I noticed, were clutching the sides of her desk. Knuckles so white, they looked like naked bone instead of skin. Dr. O., a patient man, slowly nodded his head, as if to encourage Alison's attempt to find words. Red splotches broke across her face. I thought she was going to cry. Instead, she coughed and ran her hands through her hair.

"My grandmother . . ." she began.

Alison revealed how her grandmother would take her and her siblings to the movies when they were young kids and warn them not to let their heads touch the theater seats if they didn't want to get cooties from the Blacks. Listening to her, I felt something drop in me that I hadn't known I'd been carrying. Alison must've felt something, too, because she sat forward and slumped over her desk as the rest of the room splintered with tension.

"Man, fuck that."

Wu-Tang and several other Black young men in the back of the room took turns shouting foul comments. Dr. O. let them. I looked at Jade. She seemed unfazed as she picked at her nails. Her back was stiff against her chair, like she'd heard it all before. Like she was determined not to slouch under the weight in the room. Jade had always irked me, but in that moment, I hated her for how she carried on in the face of such an ugly revelation. I hated her even more than I was embarrassed for Alison. I hated her because as much as I didn't want to admit it then, she was teaching me what Black resilience looked like.

---

After Alison's confession, I didn't use hair grease for a week. Every time I looked at the jars of moisturizer that left my braids smelling good and kept my scalp dandruff-free, I saw Alison as a small child, surrounded by her siblings and her grandmother, each of them making an effort to hold their heads away from the theater's seats as they stared at the movie screen.

"Girl, fuck them," Cheryl told me one day. "You keep that shit up, and you'll be walking around with lice, just like some of them."

But Cheryl started wearing more hats, I noticed. And we both avoided movie theaters during our downtime, which wasn't too hard since we were broke college kids who preferred to watch episodes of *Elimidate* and *Cheaters* in the dorms anyway. Cheryl's roommate, Nancy, often went with us on our joyrides in the woods, where we smoked weed and listened to chopped and screwed rap music. She was half Japanese, half Caucasian, and 100 percent country girl who was from a little town in the Missouri Bootheel. I trusted her, but after what Alison said in class that day, I started watching the way Nancy hit the blunt after one of us passed it to her. Was she letting the swisher paper touch her mouth? Or, with the caution of a subtle racist, did she use her thumb and forearms as a buffer to separate it from her lips?

Truth was, I could never really tell with Nancy, but my attempted observations made me more wary of others in our community as well. How did the non-Black cashiers in grocery stores and gas stations respond to me? Did they let their fingers touch mine when they handed back my change? Or were they inclined to drop loose coins onto the counter, determined not to make close contact with a Black person? Once, I witnessed a white woman refuse to use the toilet in a public restroom behind me. I washed my hands longer than usual and watched her through the mirror as she waited for another stall to become vacant—one that had been occupied by another white person.

"You're going to drive yourself nuts if that's all you ever think about," Ms. Dottie, my beautician, warned me. I'd given up on the braids that were supposed to support me while I was growing out my natural hair and during spring break, returned to St. Louis for the first perm I'd had in months. Part of me felt weak and defeated for going back to relaxed hair, but the constant paranoia of being seen as inferior and dirty after Alison's testimony in Dr. O's class wasn't getting any easier to handle. The only thing that comforted me was the fact that I outlasted Cheryl, who'd broke down and permed her own hair before college midterms. That, and having Ms. Dottie to confide in about whites' microaggressions on campus.

"You been scratching?" she asked. She stirred the white solution in the jar on her counter. "We ran out of 7-Up, so you better brace yourself. Try to keep this in as long as you can."

And I did. By the time I got to the shampoo bowl, my head was an invisible flame. Tears stung my eyes as Ms. Dottie washed out the relaxer. Wet hair clung to the open wounds on my scalp. The strong, eggy smell of sulfur made my stomach churn.

I gritted my teeth, waiting to feel acceptably clean again.

# A Girl's Youngstown

## JACQUELINE MARINO

from **Car Bombs to Cookie Tables: The Youngstown Anthology**

I used to be afraid of the mills, or what was left of them in the late 1970s. Although I grew up in Boardman, my family often went to visit my grandparents on the east side. As soon as we got to the Market Street bridge, my sister and I would hit the floor of our mother's white Oldsmobile, clasping our hands over our noses and mouths. We would hold our breath until our lungs burned, until the structures we passed turned from smokestacks to skyscrapers.

My mother, a nurse, said the pollution the mills belched into the air made people sick and turned their lungs black. We didn't doubt her. All the old people we knew died of cancer. We weren't going to let that happen to us, though. When we saw the mills, we just wouldn't *breathe*.

Youngstown residents had been passing over the Market Street bridge—most of them much more happily—since 1899. After being fought by farmers who didn't want to develop the city and "big interests" who thought the bridge would hurt them, its opening was "the climax of one of the most romantic chapters in the history of Youngstown," according to a 1914 article in the *Sunday Vindicator*. The number of homes on the south side increased from a few hundred in 1899 to several thousand fifteen years later. The number of schools more than doubled, and the number of churches increased from two to ten. Toward the twentieth century's end, however, many journeys from the south side to downtown began reluctantly in the suburbs, whose residents, like us, were drawn not for business or fun but family obligation.

My sister and I continued holding our breath over that bridge throughout the 1980s, long after the mills closed. To us, the air was toxic and always would be. Those ugly structures were like sirens warning us to get to the air raid shelter. Mom would drive fast. We'd be blue but safe.

As we got older, not breathing as we crossed into downtown became a form of protest. Going to Grandma's red brick house on South Pearl Street seemed like a form of punishment. In the house, we did little besides play poker for pennies and watch network television. Outside, my grandpa's garden took up most of the backyard, and we weren't allowed to climb the cherry tree.

Our grandparents' neighborhood was nothing like ours in Boardman. We rode our bikes everywhere, sometimes even crossing Route 224 on our own. We explored the woods with our neighborhood friends, playing hide-and-seek and climbing trees until someone was thirsty or bleeding. Our lives were full and free. Cancer, black lungs, stinky mills. None of that Youngstown would touch us. We wouldn't let it.

I didn't realize then that you don't get to choose what parts of your hometown you get to claim any more than you can choose your grandmother's green eyes or your grandfather's musical talent. You can't take the homemade cavatelli and leave the corrupt politicians, or notice the Butler but not the ruins. The Youngstown of my past is two cities: one safe, leafy, and full of promise, the other scary, dirty, and stifling. In my memories, in me, both remain.

I have lived in a half dozen cities over the past twenty years. I have appreciated and criticized them all for different reasons, but only Youngstown feels complicated. Perhaps it is complicated in the way all hometowns are. They are the places where we learn to feel love and hate and the spectrum of other meaningful emotions. But I think it's different for those of us from Youngstown. Everything about our city is heavy—steel, corruption, racial and class division and, most distinctively, the weight of others' condemnation.

Everyone carries it, even those of us without direct ties to steel or organized crime. Neither Steeltown nor Crimetown had much claim on me. My parents were professionals, and my closest relatives to toil near the blast furnace were great-uncles. As a girl, I didn't see myself in the history of Youngstown everyone else seemed to know. Where was my Youngstown? It would be many years before I would realize no one had written it yet.

At my grandparents' house, there was no thrill of discovery in exploring the trappings of my mother's past. Almost nothing from my mother's girlhood remained—perhaps because she had so little as a girl. Her tiny bedroom, at the top of a flight of steep, narrow stairs, held only a single bed and a dresser. I knew kids whose bedroom closets were bigger. There was so little room, in fact, that the door only opened about halfway before hitting the dresser. I didn't know how my mother survived in that room. My bedroom was my refuge, the place where I read and dreamed and wrote in a household where no one except for my father ever wanted to be alone.

To write fiction, Virginia Woolf said a woman needed money and a room of her own. I think that's good advice for anyone wishing to write anything, though I would add another requirement: The room should be big enough for a desk.

Growing up, my mother did not have money or a desk, and she was rarely alone. Her one-bathroom, one-thousand-square-foot house was shared with two younger brothers. My grandparents were very social, and their neighbors were close. My mother remembers their community fondly. She walked everywhere, waving at the neighbors sitting on their front porches, engaged in the traditional Youngstown pastime of street watching. She even walked to her school, Sacred Heart, with its giant crucifix that towered over the mills. In the early 1980s, however, we weren't allowed to leave grandma's brick driveway. When we went to Sacred Heart for spaghetti dinners, we drove. Its school was closed by then, and its crucifix had lost some of its majesty, overlooking the ruins of the mills we used to hide from in the Oldsmobile.

One by one, my grandparents' neighbors moved away from Pearl Street. There were break-ins and drugs. Empty liquor bottles and garbage littered the street. We rarely saw other children there—only our cousins when they were visiting from other cities.

My grandparents left for Boardman in the 1980s, and I didn't return to Pearl Street until nearly two decades later. I went back because Youngstown was haunting me. Once again, the city was at the center of something very bad on a national stage. By 2000, after a four-year investigation, the FBI had convicted dozens of people, including judges and other public officials, on corruption charges. Even its congressman, James Traficant, was being investigated.

It was like the worker uprisings of the 1910s, the mob wars of the 1960s, or the economic devastation of the 1970s. It didn't matter if you had nothing to do with any of that personally. If you were from Youngstown, you felt the heat.

Corruption in Youngstown wasn't just a one-time thing. It was "institutional," woven into the fabric of its culture. Or that's what everyone was saying, anyway. As a graduate student, I wanted to learn why. I went back to Youngstown to research the places where the city's history and my family's history intersected. I spent many hours over several months interviewing my relatives, including my grandparents. Even though I found no close relatives among the scores of Youngstown politicians, organized criminals, and lackeys who have been convicted over the years, I was amazed by the few degrees of separation between my family members and those who have given the city its disrepute.

These connections were often brief but memorable. My great-grandmother was shaken down for a gold pocket watch—the only thing of value belonging to her late husband—by a member of the Black Hand. Mobster Joseph "Fats" Aiellio, whose wife was one of my paternal grandmother's dearest friends, once gave my father a toy gun. (His mother, mortified, made him give it back.) My great-uncle Joe worked at the Calla Mar, a restaurant owned by Pittsburgh "godfather" Jimmy Prato, who threw a luncheon in honor of that grandmother when she died. At one time, almost everyone played the bug, the illegal gambling racket that perpetuated organized crime in Youngstown.

"Every day a guy would come to the house," my maternal grandmother, Betty D'Onofrio, told me. "You'd play three cents or five cents on a number."

Even I have a connection to a Youngstown criminal. Briefly in 1992, I interned for Congressman Traficant on Capitol Hill. After a full day of opening mail, answering phones, and greeting visitors, I asked one of his female aides when it would be my turn to shadow the chief of staff and attend receptions and other events, like the only other intern—a man—had been doing all day. Her answer? Never.

"The congressman always wants a woman at the front desk," she said, with a contempt I hadn't expected. If I wanted to do anything else over the next three months, she strongly advised me to find another unpaid internship.

That was my last day.

The next week, I walked into the office of the National Women's Political Caucus, a nonpartisan group that works to get women elected to public office, and asked the communications director to hire me.

She did, but only after a closed-door meeting where she told me to strike the Traficant internship from my résumé.

"He's a laughingstock," she told me. "This will follow you." Nearly a decade later, while doing graduate research, I found myself interviewing mostly women, simply because they tend to outlive the men in my family. I tried to get them to tell me more about the people they knew who factored into Youngstown's criminal past, but instead, they wanted to tell me about what their lives were like in the forties, fifties, and sixties. They told me about baking pizzas in outside brick ovens and the dangers of hanging your clothes out to dry on the clothesline in Brier Hill. (If the ash got on them, you'd have to wash them all over again.) My grandmother's family was so poor they lived off fried potatoes and whatever they could grow in the garden. Still, they prided themselves on raising good kids. Once, when my great-uncle stole a chicken, my great-grandmother said nothing.

"She just looked at him in a way that made him feel so guilty that he took it back," Grandma told me.

These family stories were entertaining, but what about the mob? The corrupt politicians? The thugs that wired car bombs and shot people? I inched the recorder closer.

"They never bothered us," she told me. "They knew we didn't have nothing."

I understand why Youngstown's wives, sisters, and daughters would want to forget the city's criminal past. It isn't really theirs; few women have emerged as perpetrators of the Crimetown, USA image. In newspaper articles, they have been inconsequential characters, lightly sketched into the background, cooking or grieving. That's not to say they didn't know what was going on in back rooms and boardrooms, but you don't take too much ownership of the power structure when you're just greeting people at the front desk.

Here were those two Youngstowns again. Instead of the free and the scary, however, I saw distinct male and female views emerge in our much-maligned city. The male one resided in the realms of collapsed industry and crime. It is the one known and vilified by the rest of the world. The female one centered on family. Though loosely referred to in references to the city's ethnic roots, its strong loyalties, and family values, that is not the story of Youngstown everyone else knows.

Despite the shame and defeatism many of us from Youngstown have felt, there is no badness in the blood here, no moral inferiority. There has been a historic lack of opportunity for half of us to speak for ourselves. Money and a room of their own? Few women in working-class Youngstown had either.

To write a creative work, according to Woolf, writers should strive for "incandescence," the state of mind in which "there is no obstacle in it, no foreign matter unconsumed." You can only get to it if you're free, even temporarily, of the emotions spawned of dependent relationships, "grudges and spites and antipathies." We don't have to let our families in our rooms where we write, but we must let them into our writing. Otherwise, no one will know our past. Steel and crime do not reflect our experience. The things we want to talk about in our eighties, those are real.

As much as I disliked going to my grandparents' house on Pearl Street, it always smelled good. I often ended up in the kitchen, where there were always hard Italian cookies that never seemed to get stale and pots of sauce or wedding soup on the stove with my grandparents bustling around them, dropping handfuls of this or that into the pots, stopping only to let us kiss their pudgy cheeks and urge us to have something to eat. My grandparents' kitchen was as loving, happy, and gender-equal as any place I have ever been, definitely worth crossing the bridge for. I am sure it was just one of many oases in a turbulent city, but not recorded or celebrated as the special thing it was.

It's a small memory, but it feels good to write about it. Finally, I can breathe.

# A Minute, A Pond, A North-Facing Window

## KIM-MARIE WALKER

from **Black in the Middle: An Anthology of the Black Midwest**

*A speck of peppa in a sea of salt,*
*This black body exists in white suburbia*
*Green-spaces with cleaner air, bike paths, and eagle flyovers*
*This black body craves existence*
*marked by miles of open sky, lakes, wildlife, and trees*
*Not blue eyes, or slow roving police cars marking*
*This black body walking round the block, cycling round lakes*
*like Becky does without hesitation*
*A speck of salt in a sea of salt*

The pond surface is half open water, half frozen over with a thin ice layer, no snow. Both stilled surfaces reflect a row of shoreline pine trees—olive green boughs with dark gray and brown trunks. Eyes on the pond, I watch stringy gray clouds inch eastward under pale blue sky.

Suddenly, the pond's mirror image captures two ravens flying overhead, flanking a hawk. I glance up to track the hawk's cruise through raven territory and down to movement on the pond. A muskrat has emerged from an edge of ice. Its silky glide ripples water toward muddy tunnels submerged on the northwest bank.

Then, incredibly, hundreds of geese in staggered V-formations fly overhead, just fifty feet above nearby cottonwood trees. A quick slide of the window lets me hear a hoarse concerto of honks and wings whooshing. For seconds, the pond mirrors feathered creatures journeying south.

Clouds pick up speed from the west. A breeze dapples the pond surface, mixes with the undulating V-wake inspired by the muskrat crossing. Sixty seconds have passed.

My heart struggles to make room for gratitude and to drop-kick midmorning's gloom. I've internalized law enforcers latest killing of an unarmed Black man and assault of an unarmed teenage Black girl, of a Black baby shot in urban crossfire. These recent events, as gut-wrenching add-ons to decades of observing how systemic institutional racism plays out on so many levels, may tip me into depression's abyss.

And though no blue-clad officer has ever touched me, my body knows invasion. I've banged my mind against a wall and there are fractures. Every millimeter crack, an instance of trying to filter human suffering. Every exuberance at being alive competes with internal screaming. Astonishing how screams erupt without sound.

From the pond's viewpoint, all that has passed overhead and through is eternal. Everlasting in the molecules and nanoparticles of elements draining into the creek into the lake and into that, which over time, evaporates to the cyclical interplay of air, water, and plant photosynthesis. All of which I'm dependent upon. Am one with.

Oneness with all things is not a choice. It is the state of existence.

Living with this paradox is hard. Me, the humanitarian and the terrorist. Citizen and police. Disrupter and critic. Consumer and polluter.

Living with this paradox is easy. Me, the pond, and the raven. Blue sky midmorning and inky star-filled night. Pond ripples and a singular wave crashing ashore.

When thoughts and words fail to marvel, this midmorning observation tilts numbness and gloom toward resilience, toward zealous activism to hold accountable each internal fracture, those long, exasperating exhales, those silent screams.

For the rest of the day, my struggle for gratitude dissolves. Sixty seconds of pond's reveal, remembered, relived.

# Marquette Park: Members Only

## GINT ARAS

from **The Chicago Neighborhood Guidebook**

My earliest memory of Marquette Park, a neighborhood embedded into Chicago Lawn—Sixty-Third to Seventy-First Streets, Western to California—is from Liths Club, a lounge on Sixty-Ninth Street. This is circa 1979, and I'm about six years old. My father and uncle sit at the bar while I occupy a table with my younger brother. We slurp RC cola, chomp barbecue chips, and watch chain-smoking men play billiards.

Liths Club belonged to Lituanica Liths, an amateur (passionate, mad, oft-relegated) soccer team of the Chicago Metro League. The strip between Western and California, Lithuanian Plaza Court, was home to over a dozen similar bars, all of which I'd visit long before finishing high school.

Between the 1960s and 1980s, the majority of homes in Marquette Park housed displaced World War II Lithuanian refugees and their children. The elders did not migrate out of economic interest or pursuit of romance; Lithuanians had fled Soviet occupation, and most ended up in America by chance. Earlier waves of Lithuanian immigrants to Chicago had set up infrastructure, naturally drawing new migrants. Certainly by 1960, though perhaps long before, Marquette Park had become the flagship Lithuanian neighborhood, boasting its own soccer team, newspapers, publishing house, bookstore, archive, teachers' academy, schools, theater troupes, opera choir, hospital, parish, bakeries, delis, and bars.

The bars were not just watering holes but community centers. Kids had their birthdays in the back rooms. Liths Club threw a Christmas party every year (I pulled Santa's beard at one to reveal my uncle's face), while another bar allowed an acting troupe to meet in the back for free, rightly assuming they'd buy a ton of drinks.

Because I was born to the displaced, neighborhood codes let me drink and smoke openly as a teen. Between the ages of sixteen and twenty, I spent the vast majority of my Saturday nights in sweaty and smoky barrooms on Sixty-Ninth, where all but two bars had the same sign on the door: "Members Only, 3 IDs needed for entrance."

Obviously, I never produced any ID. Membership was coded in exactly the way small American towns code down-home identity, though perhaps with more pathos. When the bartender survived a bombing run with your grandfather, or he knew your father had been dragged across Poland by your grandmother—the rest of the family shot in some field or deported to Siberia—he'd pour you a damn beer. The American idiocy of "underage drinking" did not beat the bonds created by collective survival, those that determined neighborhood code and custom.

The neighborhood provided cohesive comfort; everything in walking distance, no practical reason to leave. The effort to maintain culture entailed a kind of sentimentality: amber necklaces and bracelets, wooden engravings of Lithuanian castles, colorful sashes on shelves . . . all things to confirm Lithuanian identity. That one was *true*. All other shades of identity, including whatever Americanness you might have gained by birth or in transit, was a side effect of war's aftermath, more a coating than a self.

Insistence on this version of truth naturally insulated Lithuanians. Cohesion's close cousins are skepticism of strangers and paranoia of the larger world. Interlopers could find themselves walled off. Some mothers, for example, did not allow children who didn't speak Lithuanian to attend their children's parties, no matter that the Lithuanian American kids spoke mostly English among themselves. The system kept kids within fences, a long-term plot to discourage marriages to outsiders.

Perhaps the wanton teen drinking on Lithuanian Plaza Court makes more sense now? If the kids got wasted together in the safety of back rooms, in pubs whose regular drunks knew everyone's parents by name, hormones would do their thing in the safety of a controlled space. It was a variation of the arranged wedding, clannish without doubt, as Soviet occupation had this way of making you feel your culture was on the verge of being completely annihilated.

No world map showed your country—your culture existed almost exclusively to itself. When you told Americans your name was Feliksas, they'd change it in front of your face to Felix, deleting your fucking name for their own convenience. When you told Americans you were Lithuanian, they'd ask, "Is that like Russia?" You realized your family's murderer has successfully transformed you into himself in the world's mind. It left you clinging to what you had as you anointed yourself protector, handling the trauma of war in the process, something inescapable in the Lithuanian consciousness, no matter if you were born in the States, in a refugee camp, or if your mother dragged you across Poland. Lithuanians did not treat trauma by lamenting their lot in the press, talking with shrinks, or popping pills. The antidotes were prayer and church, the occasional conversation with a priest, collective weeping at funerals, or midsummer singing in backyards, wartime laments delivered in harmony to an endless flow of vodka. The mission was not to express your culture or celebrate its tones. It was to keep from dying out.

———————

Little of this registered to an outsider. Most people from outside Marquette Park, if they knew anything about its reputation, had heard it was a den of extreme bigotry, a flashpoint in the struggle for civil rights. The reputation is well-deserved.

Among the many inside jokes in *The Blues Brothers* is the satirizing of a Nazi march in Marquette Park, when Jake and Elwood announce they hate South Side Nazis and drive their rally off a bridge into the park's lagoon. In fact, fascists and racists of many stripes set up shop in Marquette Park, where various voices pronounced the neighborhood forever ethnically white, and where the Chicago Nazis had their headquarters on Seventy-First. Rallies and riots relevant to the history of class and racial struggle occurred in the park, including Martin Luther King Jr.'s well-documented 1966 visit, which was met with massive violence. That was, of course, hardly the only incident. In 1976, the National Socialist Party of America gathered to confront a group of Black protesters concerned with inequitable housing. The Ku Klux Klan staged infamous rallies, met by counterprotesters as well as cheering spectators in the summers of 1986 and 1988. The latter turned violent.

By the 1980s, the fears of white flight fed ever-more frequent accounts of violent crime.

On a Wednesday, someone's grandfather got attacked in his garage, his shelves looted of tools. The next Tuesday, someone's aunt got beaten up, her purse stolen. A friend of my college roommate came to the neighborhood to drink in one of the bars and got shot in the face as she exited her car. Her survival was pure luck.

In every single one of these cases, the perpetrators were young Black men. The stories made their way around coffee chats after church, discussed over Old Style at Plaza Pub and Gintaras Club, over cake at a Lithuanian Futurist fundraiser. The neighborhood was "being overrun." Blacks were "encroaching" from across Western Avenue, unable to remain where they "belonged." The violence wasn't a myth or raw propaganda—a woman was, indeed, shot in the face, just as friends of mine were jumped and pinned down, thugs pointing guns to their heads, demanding everything from everyone's pockets and backpacks, including car keys, cigarettes, Led Zeppelin cassettes, and a scapular, an heirloom inherited from an aunt. Residents saw real reason to fear what was happening, and no one could expect them to look to the history of American racism and housing rights to settle their dismay.

I cannot dismiss the violence in the neighborhood, though I need to stress something that bothered me in my youth, something I felt I was noticing all by myself. The diaspora Lithuanians I knew worried constantly about *them*, or *those ones*, or *juodžiai* bringing blight and violence, but it was rare to hear anyone express even vague concern over the presence of Nazis in the neighborhood—the very philosophy that had started the war from which so many had suffered.

Lithuanian racism was like an open secret. It always struck me, even as a schoolboy, that pointing out the obvious about bigotry in the diaspora often led to accusations of shock and outright denial. An uncle could go off at the dinner table, say something extreme—"Blacks should be burned just like the Jews"—but if you told someone he was a bigot, they'd gasp out, "No, no! What are you saying?" I learned racism wasn't wrong to feel. It was just wrong to admit.

I can't say how many Lithuanians carried membership cards for the NSPA or KKK, if any did at all. But let us remember that *membership* in the neighborhood was coded, abstract as the dividing line between the ghetto and Marquette Park, invisible yet ever real.

I had an experience in one of the bars that illustrates this. I must have been all of fourteen, a friend and I seated at the bar with men three times our age, our fathers among them. In the lazy buzz of barroom babble, the door creaked open and a few young Black men stepped in. They did not get two yards past the threshold when all the men at the bar turned to them to shout, nearly in unison, "Members only!" The unwelcome guests left without a word, though I doubt they looked to sociological theories to quell their resentment. I learned another code that day, one of silence. There just wasn't any reason to wonder out loud: "Oh, so that's what those signs on the doors really mean?"

That mentality became a self-fulfilling prophecy. Neighborhood crime kept increasing: battery, robbery, vandalization, even murder. Some of the old-timers looked at it as yet another invasion, another occupation, though others cautioned not to get hysterical, just to hold firm and avoid selling any homes to *those ones*. It proved impossible—not all neighbors were Lithuanian, and others just failed to feel identical shades of sentiment for the tribe. Whites fled. By the mid-1990s, the Lithuanian presence in Marquette Park was a mostly symbolic commuter culture, the delis gone, all but a few bars closed. I drank my final glass of beer on Sixty-Ninth in the summer of 1996, a day before departing Chicago for a job.

Liths Club stood as a rather stubborn nostalgia act, though it was finally razed in 2013, something I learned from a Facebook status update posted by a woman I'd neither seen nor spoken to for over two decades. Laments sounded in the post's comments, including a memorable one from a Marquette Park expat, born in the early 1970s like me, a guy suffering from illnesses related to alcohol abuse, his mental health strained by the complex childhoods we all had growing up among traumatized refugees: "Better razed than taken over by them." He meant the nonmembers, of course.

———

I returned to Marquette Park in the spring of 2018. An artist visiting from Klaipėda asked to see the old neighborhood, whose story I'd told her, so we drove down on a whim. I was sincerely curious to see what it was now. Garbage everywhere, boarded-up storefronts, barroom doors gated, their windows dirty with film. Every block had an abandoned building or two. The only active businesses, besides an old bank, were a food mart and clinic. The mart seemed primarily a liquor store, half-drunk men loitering outside, laughing and smoking. Yet with their paper bags and cigarillos, they seemed far from happy.

Wandering about, fielding unwelcome stares from the locals, we knew we were intruding, unable to claim membership to this street. Together, we sensed something we discussed on the drive home.

America—indeed, most of the West—is at a point that might be the culmination of the struggle for equality, an historical fulcrum that can see us collapse to extinction or be reborn with a new vision. The history of Marquette Park offers valuable lessons, perhaps best understood by outsiders, or those of us who have some distance from the passions.

Those of us who claimed opposite sides of Western Avenue shared much more than we could bring ourselves to see. The traumas of war and slavery are analogs, consequences of oppressive, dehumanizing philosophies that naturally leave their survivors feeling like victims. A curious note in the mentality of the victim is a sense of authority over a conflict, even a feeling that one is entirely good while others are entirely bad. Suffering can become its own drug, its own kind of indulgence, because feeling entirely good is far more pleasant than wondering what you've contributed to the madness before you. Even that question—*What role have you played in this?*—sets off snapping answers. None! I was not a slave owner. I was not a Soviet. And I am not a Nazi. I have no membership card.

The flashpoint of Marquette Park was a consequence of our inability to see both sides suffering from history's monster—families dismembered, identities rearranged, and bodies blasted across oceans. In fairness, the followers of Martin Luther King Jr. saw this with better clarity than did the residents of Marquette Park, primarily those who sympathized with the very energies that led to displacement. This aside, the question isn't who is more enlightened. The question is what codes do we want to use to determine membership to the same club. And does the survival of my club depend on a disaster befalling another?

Marquette Park used the codes of ethnicity and race. Its membership depended on a kind of paranoia that's based almost entirely on lines we're too frightened to examine. That's the lesson Marquette Park offers everyone on the outside, and the value of its history. We fear adding members to our club will kill the club's identity. That's to say, if I cannot be who I understand myself to be right now, it means I can't be anything at all. Perhaps it's time to have fewer small clubs on opposite sides of streets but extend invitations to those who've suffered from history's monster. If we count up the members of that club, we'll find it's very large.

# Rust Belt Dreams

## CONNIE SCHULTZ

from **The Cleveland Anthology**

Earlier this summer, I was talking to a stranger at an out-of-state reception when his wife walked up, bumped her hip against his, and said, "I need some cash."

"Why?" he said as he reached for his wallet.

She pointed to the bartender at the far end of a big outdoor tent. "I want to give him a tip for my drink."

Her husband fanned a few bills. She plucked two singles and he shook his head. "You don't need to tip him. He's taken care of."

I cleared my throat. "Really, he's probably not," I said, and gave a short tutorial on what my years of reporting have unearthed about unfair practices in the service industry.

"Far too often," I said, "management skims the tips."

The wife smiled, but her husband frowned. "Well, even so," he said, "guys like that know that people don't tip at these kind of things. He's not expecting it."

*So not the point,* I thought. *So not like Cleveland.*

I'm not one to romanticize the Midwest or the working class. Born and raised in both, I know we have our share of ne'er-do-wells, as my great-grandmother used to call them. But I'm smug about Cleveland, about this so-called Rust Belt full of people like me: first-generation college graduates whose lives are bigger and better because of parents who kept a promise that they would be the last to carry lunch pails to work.

When these are your roots, you're more likely to see a waitress or bartender as a human being. You can even name a relative who works in the same kind of job. You also feel an uneasy gratitude when you watch them work—wiping tables, juggling plates, and smiling at loutish customers—and see a future you managed to escape. Turns a tip into cause, which I discovered time and again in my years as a columnist for the *Plain Dealer.* Whenever I wrote about a restaurant boss taking unfair advantage of tipped employees, the reader response was swift and overwhelmingly on the side of those hourly wage earners.

In Cleveland, if you tell readers that someone is mistreating workers just because he or she can, a lot of them are going to do something about it. They're going to tip big, and in cash. They're going to call managers, too, and threaten to tell all their friends about their lousy business practices if they don't change their ways. Most people in this region want to do the right thing, and there's an untapped power for change in that singular truth.

We are our stories, which is why I'm ever faithful to this bruised and battered town. My own story begins with my parents, who raised their four kids in small-town Ashtabula but insisted that all roads worth traveling lead to Cleveland.

In our family, Cleveland was a city that kept its promises and emboldened lives. Anything related to Cleveland was bigger, bolder.

The Cleveland Electric Illuminating Company made my dad a hero in our house. For more than three decades, he worked in CEI's Ashtabula plant on Lake Erie's shore. We'd flick a switch, and my mother would say, "Your daddy made that electricity." Before you laugh, imagine a six-year-old daughter's state of wonder as she stares at the ceiling light and pictures her father harnessing a bolt of lightning with his bare hands.

Ten years later, I was a sixteen-year-old cheerleader leaping into a cartwheel when I collapsed on the gym floor during a basketball game, gasping for air. I'd been sick for weeks, misdiagnosed with bronchitis. An ambulance rushed me to a nearby hospital. It was the first of many such scary asthma attacks and long hospital stays for a disease out of control. After the third ambulance ride, our family doctor stood at the foot of my bed and said to my parents, "We've got to get her to Cleveland."

When I was admitted to the Cleveland Clinic in the early 1970s, my terrified parents finally allowed themselves to catch their own breaths. Doctors delivered cutting-edge treatment and blew wide open my small-town view of the world. Before going to the clinic, the only foreigner I'd ever met was a white South African student attending my high school through an international exchange program. Suddenly, I was meeting men and women from around the world. Some of my most enduring memories of that scary time in my life swirl around images of white coats, breathing chambers, and my father pacing as he strained to understand men with exotic accents promising that his daughter would one day run again.

I wish I remembered the name of the young clinic resident who stopped by every morning to drop off a copy of the *Plain Dealer,* then returned at the end of the day to talk about some of the stories I'd read. Looking back, I can see that he was trying to distract me from the anxi- ety that was exacerbating my asthma, but it was so intoxicating to have an adult male—a doctor, no less! —listen to me as if I had something to say.

On the day I graduated from Kent State University, my mother wiped her eyes and said, "You aren't going to leave us, are you?" She knew I was weighing my only job offer, at a newspaper in Indiana. She also knew I'd never go if she wanted me to stay.

Old story, that one. I packed up and headed to Cleveland, just as I was raised to do. Eventually, at age thirty-six, I landed at the *Plain Dealer.* It was my first and only full-time newspaper job.

If you work hard and get attention for what you do, you can get big ideas about your future and leave the place that built you. Certainly, there were moments when I—and friends who loved me—wondered if my career would be bigger and better somewhere else. Such ruminations are born of a self-importance that's bound to catch up with you. Single motherhood in my thirties was a real leveler for me. Cleveland forgave my unfaithful yearnings and pulled me through the toughest time of my life. By the time I became a columnist, I couldn't imagine living anywhere else.

Over the years, Clevelanders have had plenty of opinions about mine, but they've also made it clear that ours is a family argument. I'm grateful for the willingness of so many strangers to claim me, and I'm always trying not to let them down. Clevelanders are not shy about their expectations. One of my cherished possessions is a box full of cards and letters from readers who, on the biggest day of my career, wanted me to know they were (a) mighty proud and (b) worried that I might let the good news go to my head.

Roots matter. Without that tethering, we can lose our way, but it's also true that a tree grows only as high as its roots will allow.

For me, Cleveland has always been a place where branches tickle the sky.

# Letter to the Prodigal Son

## MARK OLIVER

**from Sweeter Voices Still: An LGBTQ Anthology from Middle America**

*Editor's note: This piece was originally published anonymously.*

I saw you standing there, all alone at the edge of the crowd. Your somber look and downcast eyes matched the slump of your shoulders. You looked defeated. It was at one of the weddings in our neighborhood earlier last year—one of those perfect early summer days before it gets so warm and humid; the scent of newly mown hay mingling with the aroma of chicken frying for the meal; the hum of conversation and laughter, and the grinding of buggy wheels over gravel as the last of the invited guests arrived. You have no idea how I wanted to walk across the barnyard and stand beside you to give you a smile and tell you you're not alone, but never before did I feel our peoples' invisible barriers of age and marital status as much as I did that evening. I didn't dare draw any attention to myself, and would not have wanted to put any more pressure on you. I tried to catch your eye, hoping I could at least give you a smile, but your eyes never left the ground. But I want you to know that I think you are brave.

When I heard you had left, there wasn't much said. You were just one of those boys who craved a life outside of our community. I assumed you'd gone for the "usual": the English clothes, the car, the music, the TV, and a life without being told what to do and how to do it. You were just one of the many who leave, and perhaps you'd be one of the ones who eventually returns. I sympathize with the ones who leave, but I understand why those who return do as well. Our life is not the easiest, maybe, but it's hard to walk away from everything and everyone you've ever known. I get it.

In time, the grapevine rustled with rumors. There was maybe more to it, some said. Then came the hushed whispers. "He lives with another man." Then there were the knowing looks, the sighs and head-shakes. "He's a gay," they whispered. And inside I cried for you. I cried for me. I know how easily I could lose it all, too, because I, too, am gay. Being found out would mean excommunication and the loss of my job, family, and friends, being "put out of the church" and "given over to the devil and all his angels."

You know how our people are. They can gossip, but when something like this happens among us, no one knows what to say, for "such things" aren't supposed to be found among us. These are situations one expects the English to deal with but not good Amish families. So many of our people don't know how to react when the "sins" they associate with "the world" appear in our own communities. But we are here. I have a few precious memories tucked away, of conversation with others who accepted me for who I am—all of me—along with a few memories from my own youth of awkward, hurried encounters in dark and quiet places in my own community.

If only I had known what you were carrying all alone. I know what it's like: the guilt, shame, fear, and despair. If only I could have had a few words with you, a chance to tell you that this is not your fault or anything that you can change. I would have wanted to put a hand on your shoulder and look you in the eye and tell you, "You are a good person. You deserve to know that. This part of you we don't understand is as much a part of you as your brown eyes or your height. Don't be ashamed of who and what you are." I would want to tell you what I so badly needed to hear when I was your age. But I didn't know. Just like you don't know about me. You and I are alike in this way. We live in a big community and are surrounded by others, yet we are alone.

I understand your wanting to leave. While others whispered and others told your parents they were lifting them up in prayer, I was hoping you'd make it on the outside; that you'd find acceptance and support; that you'd find peace. I admired your courage.

And then you came back.

Life "out there" was harder than you expected, perhaps. It's a different world, and you stepped out into it with very little awareness of how to make it. While others told your family how thankful they were to hear you'd returned and awkwardly asked how you were doing, I brushed away tears, for I hoped you could make it out there.

I hear things. I hear how your family takes you for counseling. I hear how they watch your comings and goings very closely. I hear how they plead with you to renounce your "sin" and join the church. But my pleadings are different. I would plead that you not give up, that you might use this time to make plans, that you might find the courage to leave again and that this time you'll make it. My pleading would be that you not be too hard on yourself and that you might accept yourself for who and what you are. Don't let them convince you that you should be ashamed of yourself or that you are lost and damned. My wish is to see you be able to be yourself among people who won't condemn you for what you cannot change. Part of me sees so much of my past in the struggles you are facing now. I see myself in you, and I do not want you to be looking back with pangs of regret and sadness as I now do; regret for who and what I might be had I found the courage to leave and been granted the freedom to be myself. It may be too late for me, but within, I have a strong desire to see you do what I failed to do.

I do not know why I was made this way. I do know that I didn't choose it. If renouncing my "sin" and fervent prayers could have taken this from me, it would have been lifted from my shoulders many years ago. I have finally come to accept who and what I am. The words to the German hymn I've heard countless times hit me hard the evening of that wedding: *Gott ist die Liebe, Er liebt auch mich!* (God is love, He loves me, too!) I looked across the crowd at you as they sang that evening and was deeply stirred. He loves us, too.

Please. Don't give up. Don't try to change who you are to make the church or your parents happy. Please try again. And if you can make it out in the world, know that at least one man is inwardly cheering you on. Maybe you will be the success the others coming along behind need to look up to in order to find the courage to make their own escape. Until our people change, there is very little chance to find peace among us. We preach love and forgiveness, but we refuse to forgive the ones carrying their homosexuality alone. We can forgive any number of sins but this one, and because our people won't forgive us, we must forgive ourselves.

And I ask you to forgive me. Perhaps if I had been more courageous, you might have had an example to look up to. But I failed. And I fail again in not telling you this face-to-face. But know that I am praying for you and I love you for who and what you are.

Humbly,*

---

* When this was written, I fully expected I'd always remain anonymous. I expected to remain in the shadows alone, afraid, and only able to offer encouragement from afar. I never saw it coming when I was outed, fired, evicted from my office, and threatened with conversion therapy. In those twenty minutes, my life changed in ways I'm still trying to grasp. It was the worst thing that ever happened to me but also the best. I had very little time to make a decision, but I made the only safe choice. I left. Immediately. With the clothes on my back and the few items I was allowed to grab in haste from my desk.

I'm one of the fortunate ones. I had others on the outside who were there to support me in so many ways and to make sure I landed somewhere safe. Over the next several months, I struggled badly at times. It felt like I'd lost my whole world, and in a sense I had. There were so many sleepless nights that I felt like giving up and going back. To all those who stood by me and offered encouragement, thank you. I could not have done it alone.

I know now what it is to be able to live openly and authentically. I'm in a relationship with a loving and supportive partner. The love and joy I feel with him has made the journey worth it. If all the pain and fear was the price it took to be with him as we are now, it was worth it. Steve, I love you. You are my home.

To all of those still living in fear and isolation in communities where it is not safe for you to come out, don't give up. Growth is painful. Change is painful. But there's nothing as painful as staying stuck somewhere you don't belong.

And if by some odd chance, you recognize yourself in this piece, I'm thinking of you and sending you the kindest of thoughts from this side of the fence.

# Sunup to Sundown

## VIVIAN GIBSON

### from **The Last Children of Mill Creek**

My grandmother joined many of the women on Bernard Street who left home before daylight to catch as many as three streetcars that transported them to manicured communities just west of the city limits. They arrived early to homes where they cooked and served scrambled eggs for breakfast and readied white children for school. The rest of their day was spent cooking, cleaning, and doing laundry until boarding streetcars in the evening that returned them home just in time to go to bed. Grandmama said that there were sundown laws that mandated people of color to be off the streets in the county by sunset. If she had to work late, her "white folks" (that's how she referred to her employers) would drive her to the Wellston Loop to catch an eastbound streetcar back into the city.

My grandmother was in bed for the night by 7:30, which was our time to be quiet. A slammed front door, a burst of laughter, or the rhythmic thumps of Sam Cooke singing "Another Saturday night and I ain't got nobody" on the radio would elicit familiar rapping on her bedroom floor. There was a broomstick leaning against the wall—an arm's length from her bed—just for the purpose of pounding a signal for silence. Sometimes, out of frustration, she would shuffle in her well-worn slippers to the top of the stairs and call down to my mother, in a commanding tone made no less threatening by her shaky, weary voice: "Frances, make those children be quiet." It usually worked for the rest of the evening.

Halfway up the stairs that led to Grandmama's rooms was my favorite retreat from the constant hum made by the ten people inhabiting the three small rooms below. The worn wooden risers and treads of the steps created a perfect work desk for cutting out Betsy McCall paper dolls. The eagerly anticipated monthly issue of *McCall's* magazine provided me with hours of cutting out brightly colored paper dresses, coats, and hats that I carefully crimped onto Betsy's posed body. More hours were spent drawing new outfits of my own design. Using the smooth white cardboard that formed Daddy's freshly laundered Sunday shirts into a starched folded rectangle,

I cut and crafted small easels that held my paper dolls erect for miniature fashion shows.

That space that divided Grandmama's quiet from our constant hum held another appeal for me—it was an opportunity to eavesdrop on my grandmother's cloistered existence just feet away. There was always a low murmur from the brown molded-plastic Zenith radio that sat on the crowded table just inside her bedroom door. The black rotary telephone that took up most of the remaining space on the small table rarely rang in the evening. But when it did, I leaned in and pressed the side of my face against the upright wooden balusters and positioned an ear to hear what was said. Sometimes I could tell it was one of the sisters from the church, usually Mother Vine. Mother Vine was a feisty and friendly old lady who always smiled and stroked my face on Sunday mornings when we arrived at the church. She tilted my chin upward and looked me in my eyes in a way that my grandmother never did. She would always ask, "How's yo' mama?" as if to distract me while she magically presented a peppermint candy from her purse. I couldn't see Grandmama's face, but I could hear a slight smile in her voice after she said, "Hey, Vine." Their phone conversations never lasted long and ended with a wry, knowing chuckle followed by, "You get some rest now, bye."

Other times when the phone rang, I would hear a voice and words that I hardly recognized. Her side of the phone conversation started with the usual questioning "Hello?" then changed to an unfamiliar subservient "Yes, ma'am." After a pause, her voice changed again to a soothing, maternal tone that I only heard during these exchanges. "I know," she'd say reassuringly. "You be a good boy now. Go to bed, and I'll be there when you wake up in the mornin."

# How to Be Midwestern

### PHIL CHRISTMAN

from **How to Be Normal**

I think nothing has shadowed my development as a writer more than my failure to have an interesting childhood. Most of it I spent watching TV. My family was kind of poor, but our poverty was more of a chronic than acute condition. It was the kind of working-poor experience that leaves you with a pervasive sense of limitedness and an instinctive terror of bank tellers, but not the kind that, once survived, makes you sound badass and inspiring. As for adolescence, my main memory of it is a pervasive boredom and a sense that interesting things only happened elsewhere and to other people, that I was doomed forever to be entering rooms moments after someone had said something funny or cool, learning about a party on the following Monday, befriending a group of people only long after its best anecdotes—"Remember when we climbed on top of the middle school and the cops chased us?" "Remember when we tricked those freshmen into smoking parsley?"—were already long established.

I felt about my hometown the way a person with only one book comes to feel about that book. Maybe it's a very large book. Maybe it's an almanac! Still, sooner or later, its familiarity becomes more alarming than reassuring. You feel sick of knowing every paragraph, oppressed by the possibility that the world is actually small enough to fit within your head. The sense of an unchanging everydayness was so strong that it became like a kind of depression.

Looking back, I can assign many causes to these feelings of everydayness and belatedness. I can chalk them up to economics or to family trauma—the abuse my father experienced and the smallness of the world he built himself in response. I can talk about undiagnosed depression. I can cite the limitations of my family's worldview, the kind of Christian fundamentalism that, by answering every question with a Bible verse, extinguishes the sense that there can be any mystery or undecidedness in things, a case of religion as, actually, the death of religious feeling. But I didn't have any of these explanations at the time, and, as will be seen, I probably don't fully believe them even now that they're available. All I felt was the heaviness.

———————

In adolescence, to relieve this heaviness, I ran. When I ran, it was as if the map of the place that existed in my head got rearranged, reordered. I knew where every road ended and every intersection happened, but when I ran, I felt as though I didn't know these things anymore. Every square on the map was somehow heightened, every familiar house strangely lit up or shadowed. I would run long, till that map was obliterated, and then I'd run back, like a dog with one of those electronic collars.

When I think of what the Midwest gave to my imagination, I think first of the way this landscape suddenly shifted in those moments, the way I suddenly felt that I didn't know it. It's not only the flatness that writers like Michael Martone and Marilynne Robinson have described so well— how it makes the world into a kind of showcase or theater of the glory of God or of humankind or of the inexplicable—but a duality. You're looking at a flat field, a thing that just lies there, that has nothing to do but be patently itself, and you suddenly realize that this flat square is also more things than you can possibly fully see at once. By laying itself out for you, it also exhausts your seeing and forces you to confront that exhaustion. It reminds you how little you see of what you see. And this estrangement doubles back on oneself. You know the truth of Willa Cather's famous sentence, "Between that earth and that sky I felt erased, blotted out." What even are you, anyway?

It's the sense of a sudden toggling between a picture that is indescribable in its banality and one that is indescribable because it is too strange and complex to fully absorb—this is probably the single thing that is most important to me as a writer. The idea that mystery doesn't have to be sought, just noticed. That we are not terminally disenchanted beings roaming a landscape of atomization and anomie. That everything, as my hero Marilynne Robinson has also said, always bears looking into. That we "know" our landscapes or our jobs or our selves as we know our family members—that is, in a way that absolutely does not preclude those destabilizing but also beautiful moments in which we sigh and say, "Did I ever really know her?" My favorite writers—and a lot of them tend to be midwesterners—are people who can make a reader not so much doubt as forget the map of the world that they carry in their heads. These writers take it that the obvious description is the wrong one.

I believe in that with religious intensity, and it makes writing hard. It also makes living hard. I fear the obvious so much that my evasions of it have sometimes made me ridiculous, so determined was I to find the complex secret meaning behind my own or someone else's feelings or behavior. As an example, I once had a roommate who drank alcohol constantly, insisted he wasn't an alcoholic, and stole a twenty off my dresser to buy alcohol. So naturally I agreed with him that he wasn't an alcoholic. It would be reductive and limiting to reduce someone to such a loaded term, to put the species ahead of the variation once again. He was not an alcoholic. He was, like all beings, a one-off, a miracle, an unrepeatable microtone in an infinite harmonic scale. Indeed. But he was also an alcoholic, and I needed that twenty.

You could almost call it the counter-satirical impulse, insofar as classical satire consists of reducing everything to the most ridiculous possible version of itself and then smashing these stock figures into each other at high speeds so that when the dust clears, nothing is left but the status quo ante. I recently read, for the first time, a novel that I had always heard described as a kind of satirical vision of the Midwest, Evan S. Connell's *Mrs. Bridge*. It is set in Kansas City between World War I and World War II and is written in tiny vignettes, between a paragraph and a few pages long, each of which has an ironic or sardonic or merely neutral title. This is a description of the titular character running into a well-known acquaintance:

> On a downtown street just outside a department store a man said something to her. She ignored him. But at that moment the crowd closed them in together.
>
> "How do you do?" he said, smiling and touching his hat.
>
> She saw that he was a man of about fifty with silvery hair and rather satanic ears.
>
> His face became red and he laughed awkwardly. "I'm Gladys Schmidt's husband."
>
> "Oh, for Heaven's sake!" Mrs. Bridge exclaimed. "I didn't recognize you."

The title tells us why this is funny: NEVER SPEAK TO STRANGE MEN. The point, of course, is that all men are strange; only context makes us think otherwise.

Now, this is a comic passage in a book that is frequently very funny, but the comedy is in unknowing: the fact that Mrs. Bridge can't recognize someone she has known for decades. That is the joke at the heart of the novel as well: that everybody is strange to Mrs. Bridge, and she, in turn, is a stranger to everybody. Nobody, not her children, not her husband, nor even herself, knows her. As the book's first sentence tells us, she is "never able to get used to" the sound of her own first name. The comedy of the book is precisely not satirical in the sense of reducing Mrs. Bridge or Mr. Bridge or the other characters to types at whom we are invited to laugh. The comedy is in the gap between their characters on the one hand and the strategies they use to understand each other on the other. Mrs. Bridge is often described as a middle-class housewife, and when you put down the book, you want never again to hear the words "middle-class" or "housewife." You want words that open up rather than words that settle.

———————

Such as it is, this is my poetics. It's nothing too fancy—a person in a satirical mood might say it's just a little Russian Formalist defamiliarization with a bit of mainline Protestant uplift thrown in. It's also my politics and my ethics, such as those are. I try not to understand my students too quickly; I try not to thrust limiting assumptions on other people; I try to let people surprise me. I mostly fail at these things, and sometimes they feel irrelevant in a historical moment when so much of the evil around us is unsubtle and simple. But by that same token, if there is any hope for those who live in such a moment, it is precisely where, to my mind, literature and beauty have always resided: in the part that isn't obvious, in the part you can't see though it is right in front of you, in the calm mystery of what is.

# CHANGING
# TIMES

---

# "The Projects":
# Lost Public Housing Towers of the Midwest

## MICHAEL R. ALLEN

from **Midwest Architecture Journeys**

When I was thirteen years old, I was standing next to a public housing tower at the Darst-Webbe Apartments in St. Louis, photographing the abandoned City Hospital, when a rock struck next to me on the sidewalk. A teenaged boy shouted at me from a mesh-enclosed gallery between two brick-clad slab sections that were part of a Y-shaped tower. This was one of seven towers that composed the project, designed by Hellmuth, Obata, and Kassabaum and completed in 1960.

I looked up at the stark, unadorned buff brick walls, the small window openings, the open vertical galleries with stained and multiple-times-painted metal mesh guards. I'd never really recognized modernist architecture before, but these buildings began to dawn on me as something alien to the vernacular city. Later, I would read the words of architectural historians like Vincent Scully, who castigated such buildings as part of American urban renewal's "bureaucratized and brutalized phase." Most writers were even less generous. The towers were "the projects," shameful and failed architecture eviscerated from the canon of American modernism.

Yet at the time I first noticed the towers, around 1994, people were fighting fiercely to save Darst-Webbe—architectural merit be damned. Its towers would be gone within just seven years, replaced by a different kind of housing project. The sturdy brick towers, which vibrantly proclaimed both an architectural modernism and a staunch service to residents, disappeared as the federal HOPE VI (Housing Opportunities for Everyone) program claimed Darst-Webbe and many more high-rise public housing projects nationwide. HOPE VI did not require one-for-one truly public unit replacement, and residents went to federal court—unsuccessfully—to retain the 1,225 units of public housing at Darst-Webbe.

Darst-Webbe was gone by 1999, and today its super-blocks have been carved into a semblance of traditional urbanism, although with strange jogs, dead ends, and park mall sections to its streets. The streets are lined with a jumbled assemblage of buildings with strange clip-on details, obviously veneer brick cladding, and ominously fenced side and rear yards. The landscape is lushly planted, but with a homogenous palette of plants straight out of a garden catalog. Few people are out front of buildings, and none of the buildings or lawns give any clues who lives here. Strangely, the old Darst-Webbe landscape, with its stark and unplanted lawns and open parking lots—the work of landscape architect and Washington University professor Emmet Layton—seemed more evocative of residents' identities.

By the time of Darst-Webbe's demise, HOPE VI had already decided the fate of St. Louis's other high-rise public housing developments—with other midwestern cities like Chicago in the works for clearance and replacement as well. These modernist towers once defined the centers of cities, forcefully aligned with the urban renewal freeway system. No one could approach the inner-city areas of St. Louis or Chicago without confronting clusters of nearly identical towers that gave architectural modernism its staunchest—and most controversial—presence in the urban landscape. Today, only a handful of outliers remain in the Midwest, including Ralph Rapson's Riverside Plaza (1973) in Minneapolis, whose six buildings forcefully impact many views of the city. Yet Rapson's artful details, including colored panels, soften the tower forms. Old towers like Darst-Webbe were value-engineered down to basics—down to the most elemental interpretation of architect Adolf Loos's axiom that "ornament is crime."

These towers, of course, had symbolized the ills of architecture and public policy since the Department of Housing and Urban Development (HUD) had initiated the demolition of the massive St. Louis project of Pruitt-Igoe, with three towers brought down in 1972 and the remaining thirty leveled in 1976. Pruitt-Igoe, riddled with crime, broken pipes, and trash-strewn corridors, came to symbolize the failure of new architecture to remedy the ancient ill of urban poverty. The spree of high-rise demolitions that followed would only confirm the fact, not rebuke it.

Yet Pruitt-Igoe had been an endemic part of the St. Louis skyline, and rightly so. Its sleek, modern brick high-rises often take a beating for embodying Le Corbusier's ideal of the *ville radieuse*, while in fact they were a compromise between architectural idealism and bureaucratic pragmatism. The 1949 United States Housing Act funded Pruitt-Igoe as part of a wave of similar urban public housing projects. The federal government had never directly funded housing project construction but instead had provided financing that had to be remunerated. The 1949 Housing Act defined a robust federal involvement in housing poor and working people—a provision that accompanied a resounding inflation of mortgage guarantees for new homes segregated racially to whites and spatially to suburbs.

The Public Housing Administration (PHA) favored standardized high-rise building types—a radical, massive version of Corbusier's tower in the park—for their capacity to rehouse large numbers of people, and their supposed cost efficiencies. But there was nothing utopian about American public housing modernism. It represented efficiency and a break with the image of the historic slum, and architects ended up dictated by, rather than dictating to, federal and local bureaucrats.

Pruitt-Igoe's lead architect, Minoru Yamasaki, at first fought any plan for modular high-rise buildings, urging instead a cluster of mixed-rise structures. But when the precursor to HUD forced Yamasaki to embrace two standardized eleven-story building types, the architect delved into modernist and vernacular traditions to sculpt an environment of thirty-three buildings with many overlooked features.

The towers at Pruitt-Igoe, completed by 1956, had south-facing, open, windowed galleries that admitted lots of light. Their skip-stop elevators attempted to encourage social interaction by limiting easy walks from elevator to apartment doors—some people had to walk stairs and meet neighbors along the way. The landscape below featured playgrounds and eventually a public library, community center, and gym. By the 1960s, the St. Louis Housing Authority had a very detailed and strong landscape plan prepared in part by Harland Bartholomew Associates, which was never fully implemented. Still, Pruitt-Igoe had, through intent and execution, benefited from clear and deliberate attention to the design challenges the project posed. Similar ideas worked in other parts of the world, such as Brazil and Yugoslavia, making the indictment of modernist design as the fundamental flaw a glaring occurrence of American lack of self-awareness.

Along with Pruitt-Igoe, the most extreme examples of the new public housing project design were Chicago's Robert Taylor Homes and Cabrini-Green. The Taylor Homes consisted of a regimented landscape of twenty-eight sixteen-story double-loaded corridor towers—adjacent to the eight-tower Stateway Gardens project—that made Pruitt-Igoe seem almost plutocratic by comparison. Designed by Shaw, Metz, and Associates, the towers encompassed 4,415 units, making the Taylor Homes the largest single project funded by the 1949 United States Housing Act. The lines of these towers for years ran for more than two miles along the Dan Ryan Expressway, south of the city's downtown core. While the Taylor Homes died in infamy, their forms actually balanced expansive urban views with a counterpart providing poor people with the same luxurious scene—just as Pruitt-Igoe was called the "poor man's penthouse" in early years.

Larger than the Taylor Homes, and even more notorious, was Chicago's sprawling Near North Side complex of Cabrini-Green. The project actually evolved in ten stages from 1942 to 1962 and was a collection of adjacent projects rather than one single project. The Frances Cabrini row houses were fifty-four low-slung, two-story buildings; a later extension added fifteen redbrick low- and mid-rise buildings. The William Green high-rise towers, designed by Pace Associates, consisted of fifteen-story double-loaded slabs with redbrick cladding set into an exposed white concrete grid. These towers, known as "the whites," became potent national symbols of public housing, perhaps even more than Pruitt-Igoe's towers. A more favorable view was disseminated by Norman Lear's Cabrini-based sitcom *Good Times* (1974–79), the only US network television show set at a public housing project.

Yet Cabrini-Green already possessed a divided symbolism by the time of *Good Times*. Architecture critic Lee Bey writes that daily life at Cabrini-Green by the 1980s often produced "sudden and unspeakable cruelty and violence." The deterioration of conditions led Mayor Jane Byrne to move into the project for twenty-five days in 1981, although her embrace of the project did not alleviate its problems significantly. Toward the end of its days, Cabrini-Green was known notoriously for the chilling tale of Girl X, a nine-year-old girl raped, beaten, and left to die in one of the tower stairwells. Modernism began to seem culpable, with its alien-built forms mirroring a social alienation of life within.

Mostly, the public narrative of life at Cabrini-Green, the Taylor Homes, Pruitt-Igoe, and other public housing projects perpetuated the same narrative about the slums they replaced. The synchronic conclusion of politicians, reporters, sociologists, and architects was predictable, because it was the same as the one reached about the old slums: the physical environment of the slums needed to be eradicated. Rarely did the narrative account for the paucity of resources given to residents for their own success, or the fact that federal housing money could only fund tower construction, not critical maintenance. The perception of the towers' ugliness allowed for a substitute target to replace the fundamental superstructure of human poverty.

The achievements of the towers in delivering fireproof dwellings with central heat and plumbing, the features like beautiful upper-floor views and open play areas, the durability of the buildings that made them ripe for rehabilitation—all were immolated on the pyre of blame. Under the administrations of presidents George H. W. Bush and Bill Clinton, the seed of antagonism toward towers germinated into HOPE VI. Along the way, though, the federal commitment toward direct provision of housing withered and lagged into a guarantee of a semi-privatized program that reduced housing units and introduced private profits.

It seems too obvious to note that the HOPE VI regime has replaced a series of pungent, durable architectural forms with timid buildings designed to last less than fifty years. In the breach between these modes of providing public housing lies an attendant diminution of resources for public housing, rather than any meaningful reform. Thus, midwestern cities are left with a more palatable era of public housing ahead of an impending crisis—when the brick veneer-clad platform frames of the replacement housing start to fall apart with even less available federal money for repair and replacement.

As awful as life at the towers may have been, and as disreputable—if not sinister—their forms became, they represented a real investment in the lives of poor people. They provided a rupture from traditional urban forms, allowing cities space to resolve whether more responsive architecture with modern amenities could make a difference in the lives of working people. Of course, the towers failed to solve problems of wealth, education, and happiness, but not necessarily by design. Architects like Minoru Yamasaki involved in public housing design ultimately had too little power in shaping their forms and details, not too much. Yamasaki even privately predicted Pruitt-Igoe's failings after losing battles with PHA for a plan with fewer towers, which he thought needed balance to produce a livable human environment.

Walking past the chain stores where Cabrini-Green once stood, or the plasticine streets south of downtown St. Louis where rocks were cast from high-rises by errant teens, one can envision the inability of architecture to work magic without any concomitant change in public policies related to health, education, and welfare. One also sees that the American psychosis of race still stands in the way of meaningful change. The towers were easy scapegoats for a society unwilling to give its resources directly to human needs but always willing to build monuments to its own virtue.

Someday, perhaps, when the replacement housing fails, urban governments will confront the roots of poverty that Pruitt-Igoe neither confronted nor exacerbated. When that day arrives, however, the federal government that forced cities to build giant boxes, then to demolish and replace them, will likely evade any further assistance on a large scale. Already, under HUD Secretary Ben Carson, HUD is shutting down rather than repairing buildings with maintenance problems. Neither the Republican nor the Democratic party champions public housing any longer, as both parties rely on market liberalism to resolve housing shortages.

The missing towers in Chicago and St. Louis evoke the "Pruitt-Igoe myth" that urban designer Katherine Bristol identified years ago but raise it some. The most dangerous myth about public housing is that it no longer is the public's responsibility—that architecture, once blamed for social ills, now has become neglected altogether in our discourse, because now we simply blame government intervention. The Right stands by a libertarian bootstrap version of the myth, while the liberal Left has its own anarchic construct that holds the systemic racism of the federal government (still not vanquished) as reason to not trust any future perfection. Both sides of the ruling ideology seem aligned in a quest against any future public housing.

Architecture, if exonerated, could resume the quest for new forms that might house people without destroying urban fabric. A new era of public housing ought to be in force, especially as precarity rocks the US labor market. Instead we cower behind policies that took the lapses of modernism as cover for gutting public housing and terminating any further possible architectural experiments. The Midwest deserves to reverse both, so that it can once again make visible and daring forms of care for everyone. As daggers of hyper-capitalist luxury housing rise in Chicago, Minneapolis, St. Louis, and elsewhere, replacing the order of care for the poorest with the exaggerated presence of the wealthiest, the moment calls out loudly.

# Pilgrim on the Interstate

## NARTANA PREMACHANDRA

from **The St. Louis Anthology**

I awoke in a state of shock on Thursday, March 5, 2015.

Even though I was prepared for the events of that day, the full, daunting significance of what was about to happen only revealed itself to me as I entered waking consciousness that morning.

"From this day forward," I thought, sitting up on my bed, "I will no longer have access to a Cadillac."

It was true. After forty-six years of having my father's Cadillac always at the ready to take me where I needed to go, I would no longer have access to that glorious icon of American engineering, creativity, and radiant, no-excuse panache. We were selling it today.

My father had died the previous December, unexpectedly; and while we would've loved to have kept his car, it was simply not practical.

Even though I had driven his car now and then, I never felt comfortable driving such a big car for daily errands. As my Chilean friends put it, when they sat inside the comfortable vehicle for the very first time, "It's like a living room in here."

Plus, we couldn't afford all the expenses that went along with keeping the car—auto insurance and property tax, two of the banes of keeping a car of one's own. Not to mention, of course, upkeep.

And thirdly—and perhaps most significantly—this 2007 Cadillac DTS was his. Ever since he bought his first car of the legendary lineage in 1964—a Cadillac DeVille, with a body sleek, long, and black (and bearing a modified tail fin)—he always drove Cadillacs.

My dad drove that fine car constantly, as he picked up blood specimens from doctors' clinics to analyze in his thyroid specialty lab in south St. Louis County. One of his clinics was in St. Peters, a good half hour outside of St. Louis, across the Missouri River. He went there twice or thrice a week for years; I used to wonder when his weekly pilgrimages to St. Peters would end. While he was an expert driver, I naturally worried a bit about him as he grew older.

In the end, his weekly rounds to St. Peters ended in a way I'd never imagine.

——————

My mother arrived in the United States on November 22, 1963. The day John F. Kennedy was shot.

She heard the news before my dad, in what was still Idlewild Airport in New York City. My dad had gone to claim their baggage. A woman from the Philippines was seated in a chair next to her, crying. She too had just arrived in the United States, and it seemed as if she already missed her homeland.

My mother noticed an outburst of chatter. Then someone pasted a piece of paper on the wall:

**President Kennedy has been assassinated.**

She told my father, who didn't believe her; he thought it was a joke in poor taste.

Later, my dad, a medical researcher specializing in the endocrine system, who went to his lab seven days a week, who worked until a few days before he died, who believed wholeheartedly in the fail-safe formula of faith, prayer, and hard work, stayed home from his lab to watch President Kennedy's funeral on the television.

On his desk still sits a plaque: "Ask not what your country can do for you, but what you can do for your country."

Not only did my dad contribute greatly to pure science—researching the thyroid gland and the endocrine system and their relations to diabetes and aspects of gerontology, among other avenues of interest—he and my mother began a classical Indian dance company, Dances of India, in 1977. It celebrated its fortieth season in 2017–2018. This is a milestone for a minority arts company in the Midwest.

As anyone in the arts knows, you can't "plan" for your dance company—or your film, or your novel—to break through, gain respect from the community, and be around for decades. My mother once said, reflecting upon four decades of leading the premier classical Indian dance company in St. Louis, "It just happened."

That's the thing about destiny—it just happens. For I'm certain that when my dad came to the US, he never imagined that in between his trips to his lab, he'd drive his family around for dance performances—not simply around St. Louis and Missouri but as far afield as New York City. It is hard to believe now, but in the 1980s, there weren't enough Indian performing arts companies in NYC to participate in a Festival of India, so the organizers invited us to come. And we did—in Dad's Cadillac.

But my dad didn't consider driving his wife, daughter, and students around the country a hassle.

Why not? Certainly, he had developed a deep respect for dance since marrying my mother. He had never been exposed to dance in his own family; once he saw my mother perform Bharata Natyam, he realized how much dedication and discipline it took to not simply learn this traditional art but to perfect it.

But there was another reason. It's the reason he—this soft-spoken South Indian scientist—treasured his Cadillac.

He loved to drive.

And he loved the interstates. He drove across wide swaths of America without a cellphone or GPS for decades. Once, he told me, his tire blew out somewhere in Missouri—I think—and he landed in a ditch. From then on, he learned how to maneuver the car carefully for any eventuality.

He first arrived in North America in 1956, the same year the Federal Aid Highway Act was signed, inaugurating the birth of the interstate. His life here developed alongside the establishment—not just the dream, but the *manifestation*—of the eternal road. As President Eisenhower put it, in a speech in Cadillac Square, Michigan, in 1954:

> We are pushing ahead with a great road program, a road program that will take this Nation out of its antiquated shackles of secondary roads all over this country and give us the types of highways that we need for this great mass of motor vehicles. It will be a nation of great prosperity, but will be more than that: it will be a nation that is going ahead every day.

I can only wonder at the excitement my dad felt, arriving in the United States at such an exhilarating point in time, a time when the country was doing all it could to expand one's frontiers.

———————

How much did my dad love his Cadillac? He loved it so much he once shipped it to India in the 1960s to show to his relatives. My grandmother wrote in her journal, "Oh boy! It was a sensation when the car passed thru on the roads . . . the policeman at the circle instead of giving signals would get stunned and stand in a rigid pose."

The Cadillac—chariot of Marilyn Monroe and Jackie O., muse of Elvis Presley and Bruce Springsteen—was now a traveling home for a family of South Indian Iyengar Brahmins from Bangalore, a town of which few in the United States had ever heard.

How could they have heard of Bangalore, when they had barely heard of India?

As I was growing up in the 1970s and 1980s in St. Louis, my family and I often received the question, "Where are you from?" And every time we said we were Indian, or even that we were from India, well, that was a mistake. For people—men and women, young and old—always, always responded excitedly, saying, "Really? I'm a quarter-Cherokee!"

Sometimes we just laughed it off and didn't say anything, and sometimes we tried to emphasize that no, we were from a country called India, which didn't necessarily clarify the confusion caused by Chris Columbus's colossal error of geography. Once in a while, however, when the fog did lift, we'd receive responses along the lines of, "Wow. India. It must be hot there." Or, "India. Wow. Do you do belly dancing?"

---

Three months before he died, my dad told my cousin he was faced with a quandary—his Cadillac needed to be traded in, but he didn't like any of the new models.

I don't blame him; the newer models just don't have the élan that makes a Cadillac a Cadillac. Perhaps it was a sign. The world had changed too much. It was time to leave.

In the end, I was the one who went to his clinic in St. Peters for the last time. It was an ending to his pilgrimage I never imagined.

That morning, my dad was at home with the flu and, we would find out, pneumonia and bronchitis. He had never been sick in his life. I went to work. My mom had just had knee surgery and was in the hospital.

My stomach sank when I returned home. The house was completely dark. I ran inside. My dad was okay, just fast asleep. He had slept all day.

That night I went to St. Peters for him. We were sure he'd be back to work in a few days.

It was raining heavily as I set out on the highway. After I picked up the samples, I got back in the car to turn around and go home, and at that moment, he called me, in the middle of his exhaustion, just to make sure I wasn't lost.

It was a dark, rainy night for a girl to be out on the highway alone, after all.

---

The first person to enter our house the morning after my dad died was Amos, a maintenance supervisor at the VA Hospital at the edge of Jefferson Barracks National Cemetery, where my dad had a laboratory for thirty years. Amos, blond-haired, blue-eyed, with a sweet smile, worked on every aspect of our home for more than thirty-five years—from the sump pump down below to the roof up above.

He came over that morning because we had set up an appointment with him, a week earlier, to do some work around the house.

I told him my dad died. He couldn't speak. He just hugged me. He later was interested in buying my dad's Cadillac, "because it's Doc's." But it just didn't happen. He did do, however, a lot more work for us, and he became very protective of my mother and me.

Fourteen months to the day that I gave Amos the news of my dad's passing, there was a knock at our door.

I opened it. Amos's son.

"Dad's gone."

I was so shocked I had to sit down. Amos was only sixty-one.

Looking back on these events, I can't help but feel that somehow, the Harley-Davidson-riding, tattooed Amos and my Cadillac-driving, shirt-and-tie adorned dad, were connected deeply. As Amos's son told me, "They were like brothers."

In St. Louis County, I-170 ends. A mile before it does, there is a sign that strikes me with amazement and a frisson of fear: ALL VEHICLES MUST EXIT.

I can't believe that a grand majestic interstate can end.

But it does.

But hey, if I look hard enough, I can see Amos and my dad speeding off the interstate, away into the infinite on a Harley and a Cadillac. Nothing would please either one of them more.

And that's something to dance about.

*A version of "Pilgrim on the Interstate" was first published in* Panorama.

# Long Weekend

## BEN GWIN

From **Team Building: A Memoir about Family and the Fight for Workers' Rights**

## July 2018

On Fourth of July weekend, my girlfriend, May, and I were on our way to play pinball on the South Side when Gracie called from her grandmother's phone. When I answered, she was bawling. She struggled to catch her breath, gasping in deep sobs.

"My mom died," she said. "Come pick me up."

"I'm leaving right now."

I hung up, got in the car, and drove to Evans City, about forty-five minutes north of Pittsburgh. May's house was out of the way, so she came too. She'd only met Gracie a few times.

"She passed all her random tests," I said. "Hair tests, even. Can you beat hair tests?" May said, "I'm so sorry."

"At least Gracie is OK."

I chain-smoked my way up I-79. May counted the change in the center console and organized the glove box. I wanted to quit smoking, but that wasn't happening today. I thought back to all the times I'd driven up north when Jane and I were dating and she was staying with her mom. We were so young. I was less than a year sober and still in college. My whole life was ahead of me. Back then, she was so funny and happy. I didn't have a car at the time, so we drove around in her beat-up old Dodge hatchback and went to shows all over the East Coast. What should have been a fun fling went bad, though, when I wanted to break it off and she didn't. Then she got pregnant with Gracie.

It felt inevitable, but there was still no way to prepare for it. Ten years of struggle ended like it was nothing. Jane was gone. Some new, unknown pain would fill the empty space she left behind. The most antagonizing presence in my life, and the most important woman in my daughter's. Everyone thought she was getting her shit together. At least

Gracie got to spend a few final days with her when she was clean and in good spirits.

Jane had overdosed the first weekend after completing her court-mandated drug tests. It was the first weekend I could no longer legally keep Gracie from staying with her overnight. Ever since I'd known her, Jane struggled to stay clean when there wasn't the threat of jail or rehab hanging over her. Looking back at all the times I had talked myself into letting Jane take Gracie even though I thought she might be getting high, I felt like I had dodged an even bigger tragedy. All the horrible hypotheticals I played in my head felt certain now. Gracie's early years were suddenly different. Her mom loved her. I never doubted that. But stories of weird houses and strange men and a mom who sometimes fell asleep for no reason filled her memories, and one day, she would put all of it together. Gracie picked up on things. She was sharp.

I was heartbroken for my daughter. I was also relieved, and I felt guilty for feeling that way. I was mad at myself and at Jane. I was mad at Narcotics Anonymous for stigmatizing harm reduction and Suboxone. I was mad that our country treated addiction like a crime and not a health crisis. People kicked dope and stayed clean. People with kids who needed help got on methadone and stayed alive. Jane couldn't. It wasn't fair.

My car bottomed out and scraped the gravel when I pulled into the driveway. Gracie was waiting outside with her grandma. I helped gather her things, and we headed back to Pittsburgh. Gracie sat up front with me, and I listened as she talked and cried. I tried to focus on her and not on the added pressure we would both be facing for the indefinite future, the way we'd have to completely restructure our lives. There were no immediate plans for a funeral, but Jane's family said they would set something up later in the summer.

"I didn't say goodbye," Gracie said. "Maybe if I had stayed up to watch a movie, she wouldn't have died."

I rehashed a lot of the talks Gracie and I had after her mom went to rehab and jail and then rehab again.

"Your mom was sick," I said. "It's not your fault. It's no one's fault. We all tried to help her. I love you so much."

"I should have gotten up earlier. I could have called an ambulance." Gracie's face was red and streaked with tears. "I saw her on the floor in her uniform. Her hair was pulled back for work."

*Fuck*, I thought.

"Honey, it's not your fault," I said.

"Why did she do it? She was better. I could tell when she was high, and she was better."

This had been going on since Gracie was two years old. I'd lived in constant worry about Gracie's well-being, with only minor reprieves when Jane was institutionalized or on probation and holding down a steady job. She'd keep up appearances just long enough that I would let my guard down. Then she'd relapse again, and it would be hard to notice right away. There was always a lag, and then it snowballed, and I'd find myself trying to figure out how I'd let it go for so long. It was such a sad story to piece together backward, using only chunks from court records and police reports and the stories Gracie told me. The court system had failed all of us. I was only able to get full custody in 2015, after Jane overdosed at the playground down the street while Gracie was in her care.

Now it was over. The fentanyl-laced dope that had been killing people in the region had found its way into Jane's arm, or wherever she still had a good vein. Gracie wouldn't have to take care of her mom anymore or worry about needles laying around or worry about lying to me about what her mom had done or where they had gone. But now she didn't have a mom. Now it was a whole new thing to have to deal with. I was pretty sure Jane overdosed and died while her boyfriend was working the overnight shift at the furniture warehouse and Gracie was asleep in the next room. Or maybe Jane got high before heading out to work a double at the restaurant while her boyfriend was still asleep after working until 4:00 a.m. Gracie said she thought her mom was still alive when she saw her. She told me she had said "I love you" before she went to bed.

We'd have a lot of help in the coming months, but it was mostly just me and Gracie. That made life both simpler and more complicated. Our lives would be hard in ways that hadn't surfaced yet and that we couldn't prepare for. I'd figure out the logistics of everything eventually, but it was going to take time. Driving back to Pittsburgh with Gracie weeping in the passenger seat, even thinking about it was hard.

The next week was the Fourth of July. I had Thursday and Friday off from work, and I was entitled to three days of bereavement leave. When I went back to the office, Gracie went to stay with my parents in New Jersey. It was too hard for her to be in Pittsburgh. I tried to shuffle my schedule, and hers, to accommodate our new life as a two-person family unit. May was nonjudgmental and understanding, and I was grateful for her support.

Gracie and I didn't have much room at my place. Four months earlier, I had bought our house from my old landlord, but another tenant still lived downstairs. He was an independently wealthy consultant of some kind, and I could have charged him twice what he was paying. As it was, he paid $550 a month to rent the first floor of my house and have use of the backyard, the basement, and one parking spot. He was mostly quiet, a little twitchy. Because he had money, I naturally didn't trust him. I didn't want to be a landlord, but I didn't want to kick the guy out, money or no. So I just let him pay what amounted to less than half my mortgage and told him to start looking for a new apartment.

When I was back at work, I called HR and tried to change my health insurance, but it was hard to get a straight answer on anything. They sent me to the insurance company, who sent me back to HR. I filed multiple tickets. I thought about keeping Gracie on Jane's insurance until someone figured out Jane had died, but if I was jailed for fraud, Gracie could wind up in foster care. I tried signing up for CHIP, but my annual salary was $1,000 too high, I didn't have the proper documentation for my writing income and a number of expenses I'd written off for a book tour that was now cut short, and I had a home office that was being used less and less due to HCL's on-site only policy. If I had quit my second job, I could have qualified for an $80 per month reduction in my health insurance, but the job brought in $200 a month. I was right on the cusp, where I made too much to get any help and not enough to not have to worry about it.

If I could work from home, I could take a second job. If I couldn't, I'd have to try to work overtime. But without some flexibility, the situation would become untenable. I could live with no time or no money, but I needed one or the other. Right now, I was fucked. I was without child support, and I had to pay for Gracie's health insurance. I got the United Healthcare Gold Plan at work so her heart appointments would be more affordable. The out-of-pocket max was thousands of dollars, so I had to make sure to plan any big expenses before enrolling so I wouldn't have to worry about the deductible.

At our next monthly one-on-one meeting, I asked Donald, who had recently been promoted to team lead, if I could work from home.

"We don't do that," he said.

"Why? I need to be around my daughter. I don't need someone watching me do this work. Who do I ask? Who makes these decisions?"

"It's not something that's done," Donald mumbled. He didn't look directly at me. "I'm sorry."

"It's not your fault," I said.

We were sitting in the Raging Rapids room for our meeting. Donald was visibly uncomfortable, and I felt bad about how mad I was getting. He didn't have a say in our policies, but he also didn't seem to think there was anything wrong with the way things worked. At the end of the meeting, he told me that Lisa, the new lead analyst, would take over my one-on-one meetings.

I grabbed my laptop and went out to a balcony that overlooked the Target down the street. I felt defeated and alone. With Jane gone, I would now have to go to every event, every parent-teacher conference, and every doctor's appointment with Gracie. The Boys and Girls Club was relatively affordable, but it started to add up during the summer when Gracie stayed there all day. More importantly, I couldn't figure out how I'd support her emotionally through such a traumatic event. I blamed myself for all of it. For not doing my due diligence before I took this new job and for leaving a job that was flexible. Then I told myself I was lucky to have any job and that I was in a better situation than a lot of people. I hated feeling like a sucker. I hated that conditions at work were making my kid's life harder for no reason. But I needed the health insurance, and I couldn't quit without something else lined up. So I updated my résumé and started applying to jobs.

The next day, I went over Donald's head. I made an appointment with Nancy to work out a plan so I could better support my daughter, either by working overtime to ease the financial burden or working remotely so I could be physically present more of the time. Nancy told me Google wouldn't allow overtime, so I asked about working from home. TVCs from different vendors worked remotely. The internal Google websites said it was possible. Someone just wouldn't let us. Either Google or HCL had decided we should be on-site all the time. A manager had to put in a remote permissions request for us, and then Google could approve it.

Nancy said she'd ask Jeffrey, the deputy general manager who was never in Pittsburgh. In a week, she got back to me and said my request had been denied. I have no way of knowing if she ever asked him or if he ever asked whomever it was that made the final decision.

I'd been a contractor before with a few different companies and had always been able to talk to the person who made the decisions about my job. HCL said Google wouldn't give me more flexibility. Google's policy was that HCL had control over my working conditions and that I should go to my manager with issues. I was stuck in a loop.

In late July 2018, *Bloomberg News* published "Inside Google's Shadow Workforce," which detailed the company's increased reliance on TVCs and the disparity in working conditions between the different tiers of its workforce. It laid out everything that I'd learned firsthand since I started working at the Pittsburgh office, and it included horror stories from other TVCs about sexual harassment, health care, and the feeling of being voiceless. As the authors put it, the contract workers were "a sea of skilled laborers that fuel the $795 billion company but reap few of the benefits and opportunities available to direct employees."

After the article came out, there was lively discussion in the work chat rooms and on our coffee breaks about working conditions. A few outspoken workers said it was about time someone wrote about the fake Google jobs we all had. The old guard at HCL in Pittsburgh knew what it meant to work *at* Google but not *for* Google. More articles about the inequity of the tiered workforce followed in the coming months amidst growing unrest at the company.

A lot of us were angry. We were angry at HCL and Google but also at the full-time employees who we thought were helping to perpetuate the divide between workers. The whole thing felt like a giant pyramid scheme. I decided to give it another few months to see if it got any better. Maybe I'd stay until I got my raise. I would try to power through until my life settled down, but I was still worried that I'd made a terrible mistake.

# The Burgers at Miller's (Or, Dearborn's Changed)

## TARA ROSE

from **Red State Blues: Stories from Midwestern Life on the Left**

It was the winter of 2004, at a bar and grill in Dexter, Michigan. I was quietly chewing my salad, purposely avoiding conversation with my boyfriend so I could continue eavesdropping on the discussion at the table behind me. The group included a man, his wife, and their woman friend, all middle-aged. They were chatting about my hometown thirty miles away.

"We used to love going to Miller's," said the wife as her husband and friend groaned with great longing. "Their burgers are amazing."

"Oh, the best!" the friend agreed.

They paused. I knew what was coming next, just as soon as they were thinking it.

"But you know," the husband said, "Dearborn's changed."

His wife sighed in agreement. "It used to be a real nice area."

"Those people are awful," I said to my boyfriend. I could tell from his wide-eyed glance that, even if he'd been eavesdropping along with me, he wouldn't have deciphered a code that had been obvious to me for decades.

When white ex-residents of my hometown sigh and say, "Dearborn's changed," what they're really saying is that it was a lovely place before the Arabs "took over." White Dearborn's pride is embodied by the towering figures of the past-world famous entrepreneur Henry Ford and longtime mayor Orville Hubbard. During his thirty-six-year tenure as mayor, Hubbard delivered an impressive array of city services, but that wasn't the only reason he was beloved by some. Hubbard died in late 1982, a few months after I began kindergarten at a public school built with Ford money. From that point forward, I got used to hearing elderly white neighbors lament the lost days of Orville's administration, "when things were different." It was always understood, without anyone needing to say so explicitly, that the olden days were better because people of color weren't tolerated.

Orville Hubbard did his best to ensure Black people stayed out of Dearborn. During his decades in office, he successfully fought against public housing, warning residents that the town would become "a black slum" if it welcomed a subsidized population. He spoke openly and often about his segregationist views, even bragging about the ways in which he'd mobilize police and firefighter sirens to harass African American residents who had the gall to break the color barrier. His legacy of anti-Black racism lived on throughout my childhood, adolescence, and all the way until I finally left town at age twenty. During the 1980s and 1990s, few Black families moved into my east Dearborn neighborhood, and those that did usually didn't stay long. But during those years, I watched the Arab community grow and prosper in the east end. And the whole time that was happening—many years before 9/11 and the widespread anti-Muslim hysteria that followed—I saw a lot of white people lose their minds over the weirdest things.

"Those Arabs smell bad."

"Look at how many of them live in a house together. Aunts, uncles, cousins, and grandparents all under one roof. Every one of those kids has a million cousins, and they'll get all of 'em to gang up on you if you cross them."

"Watch out for the boys. Don't let your daughter date one. They treat women like property. No woman in her right mind would dress like that in the summer. They're brainwashed."

"They know English. They're just being sneaky. Like how they sneak around the tax codes, and sell their gas stations from one family member to the next. It's so they never pay taxes."

Throughout my elementary and junior high school years, I got so used to hearing white people bitterly regurgitate these claims that I didn't even consider whether or not they were true. Back then, before I was aware that these stereotypes didn't hold water, I could never figure why most of these things would even make a person mad. I mean, the "treating females like garbage" part was upsetting, but I knew too many white girls from abusive families to see that as something specific to the Arab community. As for the other claims, who cares about big families living in little houses, speaking a different language, and possibly gaming the tax system?

But in junior high—when academics mean nothing and school becomes a nonstop, social-climbing death match—I noticed that even the dorkiest white kids could always cash in on whiteness. Toward the end of eighth grade, I remember walking home from school with a few of my fellow nerdy white girl classmates. We were talking about our mutual friend Jackie, who was the only Black girl in our grade. Jackie got picked on a lot, and we all agreed that some of the kids in our class were just being racist. And then one of these white girls said, "I'm not racist. I like Black people. I just hate Ay-rabs."

By this point, I'd heard so many different people, kids and adults alike, make this statement so many times it had become hackneyed. In 1991, this was what passed for a progressive mindset among white Dearbornites. You could shun the obvious racism of your parents and grandparents, yet still see yourself as superior to the "Ay-rabs." But we all knew the "A-word" was derogatory, so I called them out on it. My observation had little impact and was shrugged off quickly. Seeing themselves as superior to Arabs wasn't the point of the discussion. It was just an afterthought.

In high school, I met and began dating Sam, who was the only Arab in my hipster friend group. At our largely Arab American high school, hipsters—aka "alternative" kids—were not considered cool. But he was quite the tastemaker among us weirdos, with his blue hair, flannel shirts, Doc Martens, and antiestablishment column in the school newspaper. The thing our alternative pals didn't always understand was that Sam came from a long line of hardcore leftist, antiracist activists, and he wasn't interested in being deemed worthy by our white standards.

I can still see the withering expression on his face when one of the guys in our after-school theater group said, "I hate Ay-rabs, except Sam. He's not one of them. He's one of us."

"Hey, don't say that," said Sam.

"Say what?"

"Ay-rab."

"Oh. Sorry, man."

Sam later told me in private how much that guy pissed him off, how he could somehow see Sam as "not one of them." Indeed, when it came to the alternative crowd bagging on the rest of the student body, it wasn't always easy to tell where a healthy hatred of the popular kids ended and anti-Arab racism began. Because at my high school, Arab American culture had become the standard for what was considered cool. While those in my social group (and at the whiter high schools across town) were embracing grunge rock, most of the student body enjoyed Middle Eastern pop and freestyle dance music. Secular girls wore their hair big, while religious girls wore hijabs. Boys favored slicked back manes, black leather jackets, and heavy cologne. Many of the white kids mimicked the secular Arab trends because that's what was fashionable. For my mostly white alternative crowd, resenting the dominant culture meant resenting the things Arabs celebrated.

But I was used to being an outsider with weird taste and didn't mind being different. By junior year, I figured out that most classmates who teased me were just messing around, and some of their jokes were pretty hysterical. If I could maintain a sense of humor about myself, I'd be fine. So I learned to relax. High school still felt endless and boring as hell, but at least I no longer suspected the more "normal" kids were out to get me. It also helped that I was spared the usual conventions of high school misery. I was one of the weird weed-smoking, sex-having kids in a school where there was very little social pressure to do these things. If I'd been trying to fit in with a more conservative crowd, I might have been less happy.

Even if most of the other students thought I was weird, I always knew I benefited from the unfair advantage of the teachers' favor. In the early 1990s, the white portion of the student body at my high school was dipping below 50 percent, but every single one of my teachers was Caucasian. Many of them liked me because I was studious. Some clearly preferred white students to Arabs. I knew that to them I was more "normal"—from the way I dressed, to the Catholic church I attended, to the simple fact that I spoke only that one language they knew.

Right when I was making my peace with life, I began working at the Henry Ford Centennial Library, a mid-century marble fortress located on a long strip of Ford-developed land dividing Dearborn's east and west ends. The full-time library staff consisted mainly of middle-class white ladies from the west side of town, most of whom fit a certain type: stuffy, staid, fearful, racist, and very big fans of Miller's.

I'd never heard of Miller's until I heard the librarians rave about their famous burgers. The way they fetishized it always irked me. "You've never been to Miller's?" they'd gasp, as if it were odd that I didn't hang out at a bar five miles from my house in a neighborhood I rarely visited. It's like they thought I'd missed this key rite of passage as a Dearborn person who hadn't been initiated in the cult. I automatically associated Miller's burgers with racist whites because the same people who couldn't believe I'd never eaten there also couldn't believe I actually lived in east Dearborn.

"Aren't you scared? It's so close to Detroit. I don't let my kids go there. This is as far east as I'll go. It wasn't always this way, but it's really changed.

The people have changed. The men are very rude. You see these women and girls come in here, wearing scarves on their heads. I feel so sorry for them. I can't believe there are men who still treat women that way."

On one occasion, when I heard a librarian named Connie make that last claim about young Muslim women, I thought of Maha, a girl I'd known since kindergarten who came to school wearing a hijab one day in fifth grade. I remembered Maha calmly explained to us other girls that she had a dream in which Allah told her she was ready.

"Um, I think a lot of these girls decide to wear the scarf on their own. It isn't always like someone told them what to do," I said.

"Oh, no! That's not true. They just get tricked into thinking it's their choice," Connie said with the same gentle yet self-assured firmness one uses to explain "stranger danger" to a child. I can still see Sarah, our tattooed teen girl coworker nodding in solemn agreement. What struck me most in that situation was how these two women who usually hated each other's guts were suddenly united in their shared assumption that all Muslim girls are victims. That's what I think of whenever I hear the term "white feminism."

That job was my first lesson in the way white outsiders perceived the post-white neighborhood where I was raised. And more often than not, the outsider perspective was (and still is) quite racist. But dealing with those awful white librarians had to be way worse for Sam, who worked there at the same time I did. He and I remain good friends today, and I chuckle remembering one of his observations about the 2016 presidential primary election. He compared every Republican candidate to the worst faculty members at our high school. Jeb was the bumbling guidance counselor, Rubio was the slick young science teacher, Trump was the sleazy, out-of-shape gym teacher.

"And Hillary," he said, "is every awful white woman who worked at the library."

Just days after he said that, I saw footage of Clinton in a coffee shop, sneering at a Somali-American woman who questioned her support of Black communities. "Why don't you go run for something then?" she responded to the young lady with a dismissive chuckle. The expression on her face immediately reminded me of the way some librarians would talk down to Sam. And it also reminded me of Connie and Sarah lamenting the poor, misguided hijabis. One of the perks of white feminism is that when women of color disagree with your actions or your worldview, you think you can treat them like idiot children.

A week after that Hillary video went viral, Dearborn's Arab-Americans and Muslims voted overwhelmingly for Bernie Sanders, helping him achieve his unexpected win in Michigan's primary election. Many pundits were stunned to see this community throw their support behind a Jewish candidate, but assuming the opposite result only makes sense if you also assume this community is necessarily anti-Semitic. Hillary Clinton's primary loss in Dearborn makes more sense if you consider her history of policy affecting the Middle East—from voting for war in Iraq to embracing the use of drone warfare during her tenure as secretary of state.

I've been living in the South for the past seven years, and anyone down here who's heard of Dearborn knows it mainly as a Muslim enclave. A few years ago, I met a Michigan guy at a bar in Chattanooga, Tennessee, and when I told him I was from Dearborn, I swear his immediate response was, "Dearborn's changed, huh?" Groan. I'm always quick to explain, perhaps a bit defensively, that growing up there and attending diverse schools was good for me.

But the simple fact is that I love my hometown because it's where I'm from. I spend a lot of time in Dearborn whenever I go back to visit family and friends. The familiarity of it comforts me, even the gridlike streets and cookie-cutter tract housing that I found so dull and stifling when I was young. But mostly I enjoy the people, the blunt and funny yet easygoing manners that remind me of the best parts of high school. Southeastern Michigan will always feel like home to me. Even from hundreds of miles away, I still care what happens to metro Detroit as it reimagines itself in this postindustrial economy.

So I follow news from that region, which is how I happened to notice a Twitter post from a *Detroit Free Press* journalist just days before the 2016 presidential election. "Hillary Clinton came to Dearborn today, but like her husband in March, goes to west side place, avoids mosques, Arab centers, Muslim clergy." And in the tweet quoted beneath his post were the words, "Clinton swung by Miller's bar in Dearborn, Michigan this evening."

I literally screamed. It was too perfect. I messaged Sam with a screen cap of the tweets and the words, "FUCKING MILLER'S." He replied with an "LOL." We traded jokes about the stupid, infamous burgers and the librarians who loved them. We prayed that Hillary would beat Trump anyway, but I remained bitter.

"I swear it's a dog whistle," I told my husband. And instinctively, I still believe that. Clinton took the Arab and Muslim votes for granted. She laid all her money on those white swing voters and she met them at a place that remains, to this day, a landmark for west Dearborn's shrinking white population.

I'll fully admit that I've never been to Miller's, but as far as my subconscious mind is concerned, it's a "safe space" for every white person who's ever sighed and uttered the words, "Dearborn's changed."

# Camp Dennison:
# A Hidden Gem Fading

DANI MCCLAIN

from **The Cincinnati Neighborhood Guidebook**

There's a phrase I learned a decade ago when a beloved family member had cancer and the prognosis didn't look good: "anticipatory grief." The words describe something like the opposite of longing, a pervasive sense of dread that can make you miss a person even before they're gone.

For years now, I've been grieving in advance for the neighborhood where I was raised and where I live now: Camp Dennison, Ohio. Located seventeen miles northeast of Cincinnati, Camp Dennison is surrounded by Indian Hill to the west, Old Milford and Terrace Park to the south, and Miamiville to the north, with Loveland beyond it. The Little Miami River borders us to the east. State Route 126 is the main drag through our town, which is home to just over three hundred people living in 150 households. The house where I live—a ranch built in 1937 by my maternal grandfather's maternal grandparents— sits on that stretch of road, which is alternately known as Glendale-Milford Road. (That the road shares a name with the one that runs through Evendale is a cruel trick meant to confuse anyone trying to reach our neck of the woods for the first time.)

My mom and I moved to that ranch-style home soon after her father suddenly died there in the early 1980s. I was three, and the house with its painted white clapboard and green shutters was my wonderland. My mom's seven sisters and their kids and husbands were always coming and going, as were members of our extended family who were just a short walk away. When my great-great-grandparents moved here from Milford in the 1930s, it was to be closer to their family, and by the time I came along, it still felt like kinfolk were everywhere. Weekends brought card parties, where people cussed and drank their way through games of bid whist. Summertime meant neighborhood kids playing Marco Polo in the in-ground pool my grandparents had put in the backyard, funded in part by profits from their paper route side hustle. The Gap Band or Earth and Wind and Fire provided a soundtrack while ping-pong balls whizzed across the table that was set up outside during warm months and in the living room once temperatures dropped.

Camp Dennison was the center of my world from the time I was a toddler until I left home for college. But for a long time, I was met with blank stares when I told other Cincinnatians where I was from. My answer to that tired question we ask each other, "Where'd you go to high school?" didn't make sense unless you understood how I came to be in the posh Indian Hill School District and how my mom and her sisters had before me. I didn't live in a mansion on Shawnee Run or in a cookie-cutter two-story in a Kenwood cul-de-sac. No, I was from the part of the district that gave its schools most of their Black kids. I was from the neighborhood that gave the district many of their poor and working-class white kids, too. In those years of the Reagan and Clinton administrations, the race and class dynamics of Camp Dennison flipped simple mainstream narratives on their heads. We were home to Black families with money and white families without.

On the rare occasion that I met a Cincinnatian who had heard of Camp Dennison, they would mention the Schoolhouse Restaurant, an eatery up the street that serves fried chicken and mashed potatoes on lazy Susans. My family members attended classes in that white brick building in the years before Indian Hill set up a public education system. If those who had heard of my community didn't know the restaurant, they knew of the Waldschmidt House, built in 1804 by a settler and Revolutionary War veteran from Pennsylvania named Christian Waldschmidt. He built the first paper mill west of Philadelphia around the same time. In 1861, the Union army chose New Germany (the name Waldschmidt had given his settlement) as the site of a military camp where tens of thousands of troops would go on to train and convalesce until it shut down in 1865. The Civil War–era name stuck, and occasionally, I'd meet a history buff who had come across mention of Camp Dennison while researching Harriet Beecher Stowe, the author and abolitionist who lived in Cincinnati for a while, or the Indian Hill cellars rumored to have served as way stations on the Underground Railroad.

It was a pleasant surprise when I met a Cincinnatian who knew of Camp Dennison, but their references usually felt disconnected from the place I knew and loved. To me, the Schoolhouse Restaurant's draw has never been the food but the goats who laze around the pen out back. Petting horses at Derbyshire Stables (near the intersection of Camp and

Kugler Mill Roads) and feeding goats at the Schoolhouse are part of the quintessential Camp Dennison childhood. But focusing on either place, like focusing on the early nineteenth-century homestead of a Pennsylvania Dutch settler, obscures what is to me the most interesting part of the community's history: the Black part.

Because of my family's long history here, many novels written by Toni Morrison, a fellow native Ohioan, felt familiar upon first read. *Sula*, *Paradise*, and *Song of Solomon* in particular contain snatches of stories I feel I've heard before, spoken in hushed tones at home and told only a little less artfully. A book about Camp Dennison's history published in the mid-1950s mentions the patriarch of one of the first Black families to settle in the community. "George Walton, albeit a generous man, had grown tired of donating his free services to southern plantation owners, and had joined the Union army as a cook. At the war's end he found himself in Camp Dennison where he remained and reared his children," wrote Mary Rahn Sloan. While that first sentence makes me gag every time, much of the book is a gift. Sloan describes in detail a bustling and largely integrated town of around six hundred people and a service station, grocery store, post office, active churches, and a tavern. Known in this house as "the beer garden," that tavern was across the street and is long gone, but my mom and her sisters still tell stories about the drunken shenanigans they could see from their bedroom windows.

Camp Dennison's unique history has become even more obscured in the twenty-five years between when I left for college and when a family health crisis brought me back to my childhood home last year. More white families have moved in as Black elders have sold their homes, often to young couples drawn by the promise of access to Indian Hill schools. While my childhood memories are of a neighborhood that was roughly half Black and half white, the most recent census data puts white residents at 80 percent. At the same time that the community has shifted from racially integrated to predominantly white, it's also shifting from an offbeat and remote enclave to something more like a typical east-side suburb. Growing up, I experienced Camp Dennison as distinctly rural. Unless we were on SR 126, which we called "the highway," we rode our bikes and walked down the middle of the street, confident that the infrequently passing cars would yield to us. We learned to fish on the wooded banks of the Little Miami. Our parents and grandparents tended to vegetable gardens in their spacious yards. Some of us have a country drawl I've never heard elsewhere, despite my far-flung travels. Whenever I hear my full first name pronounced "Dane-yell," I know I'm home.

These days, when I tell a fellow Cincinnatian where I live, they've usually heard of my neighborhood. That's in part because the Loveland Bike Trail is a destination for weekend warriors from all over the region. I remember when that same path through Camp Dennison was a faint dirt trail that marked what was left of the Little Miami Railroad, which was built in the late 1830s to connect Cincinnati to Springfield. As kids, we walked that path, seeking out adventures in the natural world. We called it "the tracks," though it didn't denote a divide between Black and white or rich and poor the way it often does in neighborhoods' social geographies. Now "the tracks" is one section of a seventy-mile ribbon of asphalt that carries speed demons outfitted in the latest Tour de France-inspired fashions between Lebanon and Newtown.

There's also Grand Valley, a nature preserve established on land purchased by Indian Hill in 2002. The 379-acre expanse stretches between SR 126 and the Little Miami at the northern reaches of Camp Dennison. It's where my grandfather and other men of his generation who lived here made their living, extracting the pebbles from the land and preparing them for commercial use. A new neighbor, a young woman with two kids, kept referring to all the fun they were having at "Grand Valley," and I just kept smiling and nodding, unsure what she was referring to. It has been and will always be the gravel pit to me. As Camp Dennison residents, we have access, as do people who live in Indian Hill. I recently used my mother's pass to access the gated preserve for the first time. There I saw many intrepid white people in canoes and on paddleboards. They fished, walked their dogs, or jogged along the peaceful pathways.

I don't begrudge these folks their leisure. I enjoy teaching my five-year-old to roller skate on the bike trail and skip stones on the lake down in the post-makeover gravel pit. But it's the entitlement displayed by many of these newcomers that gets me. Men on expensive bikes shout to each other as they travel in packs on the trail, seemingly oblivious to the quiet homes they're whizzing past. People with huge water toys strapped to the roofs of the cars drive by, undoubtedly readying the passes that will raise the gate to Grand Valley and grant them exclusive access to what used to be a blue-collar worksite. Do they know this history? Do they care? Athleticism and a desire for adventure bring these visitors into a community that was here long before they discovered its bucolic beauty. I grieve the disappearance of the weird hidden gem we used to be. I anticipate even more change, and, as always, letting go of the past hurts.

# Ruin and Porn

## RYAN SCAVNICKY

from **Midwest Architecture Journeys**

"A flaw ain't shit but a unique identifying mark. Everybody got a flaw. If you got a big belly, rub that motherfucker. Love it. I don't care what's wrong with you or how fucked up you think you are, somebody love your ass. So if your buck toothed? Bitch, relax. I bet there's a man in the house right now don't want nothing less than a bitch who can bite an apple through a picket fence."

—Adele Givens, *Queens of Comedy*

Cleveland is already sexy. Not to everyone, but being sexy to everyone isn't really desirable, is it? When we try to be universally sexy, we look to compensate for what we feel we lack. We get a haircut, join a gym, or get a Brazilian butt lift. We can either conform our image to the universal-basic-MTV-and-yoga-pants-at-Starbucks sexy, or we can accentuate our unique character. In doing so, one can become the object of someone's fetish. Fetish sexy is much more interesting because it contains within it some hidden or less understood desire. The Rust Belt is plagued by economic and ecological issues, but as an architectural site, it is widely considered a collection of relatively bland landscapes dotted with signature projects by a few international architects. However, Cleveland, unbeknownst to itself and to the world, is at an apex of generating one of the most desirable spaces in the architectural vocabulary. It's not just that these spaces exist but that they are being augmented and proliferated across digital space, where material, texture, scent, and sound are consumed by the power of the image. To make this legible, we have to take a close look at the industry leading the way of creating space that frames contemporary desire.

This industry is not architecture, but pornography. As always, it is one of the major industries dealing with the future of visual and interactive experiences. Virtual and augmented reality engines are currently being tested and perfected. The industry itself has moved from simply producing porn to facilitating pornographic experiences. Much like YouTube has done for video, most of the production itself is generated by a user base. The most popular category is "amateur," wherein—whatever the sexual act— the film appears to have been made outside of the studio by an everyday person in a recognizable space relatable to one's own specific desires.

Now, the most interesting shift in the industry to stem from this decentralization is the resulting Cambrian explosion of fetish categories considered desirable by various amateur directors. Porn production studios explored location early as an added aphrodisiac but never to the extent of today's sexuality market. Often enough, these locations amplify the acts themselves. This is achieved by placing the act in a greater social context. This happens in two ways. Either the act is housed somewhere in secret, relieving the viewer of the constant dread of being caught in real life, or the opposite, wherein the social disapproval of the act affords risqué locations, which increase the excitement behind the acts themselves.

For example, the desire for gay sex to achieve social acceptance leads to its portrayal in a lily-white suburban home. Meanwhile, on another website, the front seat of an automobile hosts hijinks which satisfy an urge one may sublimate with road rage during rush hour traffic. Another recently popular location can architecturally set the stage for a wide variety of fetishes—anything from a massage parlor with a secret menu, a bondage dungeon, or a wrestling arena with unspeakable victory celebrations. Framing these kinky sex scenes, to my surprise, is the familiar exposed brick, concrete floor, and rusted steel structure of a warehouse, an aesthetic I associate with the Rust Belt, well represented in Cleveland.

In asking producers in the industry why they pick such spaces, I've been informed that the warehouse is a kind of catchall aesthetic for sexual acts. It has no distinct fetish associated with it, yet it presents a highly desirable backdrop. Many backgrounds are similarly desired regardless of the acts they host—a hot tub, sports car, or rooftop garden all become actors in the scene to augment the social implications of the viewer's desire. Cleveland is home to an overabundance of this warehouse aesthetic that is considered risqué and desirable. Unfortunately, recent construction like the Flats East Bank project exemplify an easily rejected, half-baked simulation of this aesthetic. The project's most obvious design failure is its curved plan and resulting facade, which is highly inconsistent with the warehouses it's imitating. (Nevermind the sea of parking lots.) Cleveland's newer buildings often reek of the desperate desire for universal acceptance rather than confident mania. It is as bland as suburban homes yet packaged as authentic Cleveland.

Another way of fetishizing the aesthetic territories of abandonment, rust, grime, and industrial might is through a genre of photography appropriately named "ruin porn." Nomenclature aside, this photographic category typically features a first-person tour of an empty building. The movement became a documentary of the scars and relics of industrial abandonment. The resulting photographs uncover forgotten memories and forsaken relationships, yet reflect a sense of serenity and repose. The often viral photos mark an era when young Americans raised in McMansion suburban hell became entrapped by the rich imagery of despondent cities given new life through the internet.

A collapsed steel beam would elegantly cross the frame of the photograph, while the ensuing hole in the roof gave way to a bright sun shining down upon a floor covered with rubble. It wasn't just about the melancholy but the hope one found at the availability and possibilities these photographers uncovered. These buildings only needed love.

For those of us in Rust Belt suburbs, those photographs were taken only a short drive from the sterile environment that surrounded us. Looking at ruin porn photography felt like watching *The Truman Show* for the first time. What I knew as home was dramatically revealed to be a stage set where everyone was simply acting. As a suburban-raised Clevelander, I discovered that my friends and neighbors were collectively keeping a big secret: that at the heart of our pristine collection of suburbs was a putrid wasteland to be avoided completely. As a result of the burbs, the teenage angst of my generation found its way to school shootings, suicide, and drug abuse. But there were also little plots to escape the stage set, launching a grassroots return to Cleveland's gritty punk dive bars and lowly breweries in a desperate search for the remote possibility of authenticity. Yet we now find this mass return to the city is already being commodified by apartment blocks as faceless as the suburban situation we tried to leave behind. While this is typically evidence of gentrification and displacement in many large cities, with the right foresight, it is possible to plan city growth in an equitable manner. Cleveland has shown that it can stay on top of it through implements like the Evergreen Cooperatives: nationally recognized models of sustainable growth through worker and community-owned development.

Most cities have an old manufacturing area, including Vienna and Paris. Historically, the repurposing of industrial spaces for raves or gay bars has existed because those fetishes had to be kept secret. So they happened where space was cheap and out of the way, which, for well-planned cities, existed out of sight. The houses and trees that once lined the streets of neighborhoods surrounding the manufacturing areas in Cleveland are nearly fully eroded due to the massive loss in population. The result is that in Cleveland, those spaces are very much out and in the open, almost unavoidable and exposed by adjacent vacancy. And specifically, Cleveland's vast quantities of industrial spaces uniquely bend between Fordism and global post-Fordism. Many of Cleveland's companies hit a sweet spot of local manufacturing yet never fully conglomerated into a General Motors or US Steel. The resulting mutations on Cleveland's stock of warehouses is in a unique position to argue itself as among the most diversely constructed, creating repurposed magic. For example, the Seventy-Eighth Street Studios building in the Detroit-Shoreway neighborhood is the result of a rather haptic expansion of manufacturing and office spaces, producing four interconnected buildings totaling 170,000 square feet. This complex is now filled with a dizzying mix of spatial hierarchies, occupied strictly by artists' studios and galleries. In Midtown, the Mueller Lofts offer cozy living spaces in the ornate home of the "Alligator Clip" still used in electronics. This level of detail and spatial variety is lost on the tilt-up mega-warehouses of today, which would prove aesthetically and spatially inadequate for any of these conversions. The fetishization of old industrial space is a vital and underutilized aesthetic territory that Cleveland can and should claim.

What makes these buildings so desirable has little to do with manufacturing but the specific set of lyrical qualities imbued. For example, Rust Belt industrial areas feel almost quaint in comparison with the mega-production coming out of contemporary industrial facilities found in Shenzhen or Beijing. But those factories in China and elsewhere are built to handle a newer form of production. Tens of thousands of orange jumpsuits in a grid across a mighty space is a different aesthetic altogether, and it has influenced its own set of photographic explorations echoing a different and very powerful kind of sublime. Modern industrial sublime can be seen in the large photographs of Andreas Gursky. Cleveland, however, is more like the work of Gursky's contemporary, Gregory Crewdson. Crewdson eschews the modern for the weird, complex angst and multifaceted narratives made possible by America's heartland. Crewdson's photographs often have audiences asking "what happened here?" just as a warehouse conversion holds an embedded history that provokes the imagination. Cleveland is filled with bespoke buildings created before the cheap airplane-hangar suburban warehouses of today. Its heavy manufacturing history was supplemented by just enough cultural capital and craftsmanship to produce buildings that are beautifully detailed yet pockmarked by years of abuse in a way that is often beautiful and surprising. I took my fiancé on a Valentine's Day picnic in an abandoned arms factory, saw my cousin get married in what was the first American Greetings card production facility, and I went to a Catholic mass where the first electric carriage was manufactured. Some find synergy in marrying their past use with the present. In one example, the altar of said church was split down the middle by an inlaid rail line used to roll molten steel across the room to be poured. To capitalize on this culturally requires more than to embrace the fetish of grit and grime of the current urban core. In fact, the greatest challenge moving forward is in reproducing and sharing the feeling one gets when confronted with the weight of that urban core.

This is a challenge because Cleveland seems to fight against the fetishization of its professed authenticity. For example, in the inner-ring neighborhood of Ohio City, entertainment areas have flourished over the last ten years as Americans reinvent craft beer. Drinking a pint in this rejuvenated Cleveland wouldn't be the same without the gritty backdrop of the city, in much the same way a hand job isn't risky if the door is locked. When popular urban brewpubs begin expanding outward into the suburbs, this aesthetic becomes hotly contested. How can a brand-new building attempt to replicate this aesthetic? Is a pint of Great Lakes Dortmunder Ale in Crocker Park Lifestyle Center the same as it is on West Twenty-Fifth?

In researching the spread of the simulated industrial chic, it is important to look in and around Ohio but also to look in the last place that would want to be associated with harsh winters, blue-collar jobs, and sports debacles: Scottsdale, Arizona. Located in the historic old town of Scottsdale is a midwestern bar that opened its first southwest location called Two Brothers Brewing. This is a brewpub in an area marked by single-story structures architecturally gesturing to Western vernacular and drenched with imagery of the Sonoran Desert. But inside Two Brothers, one discovers an open floor plan with tall brick walls, exposed steel structures, a concrete floor, and, of course, exposed ductwork. They even had the audacity to match up the grout in the faux brick wall covering as it turns the corner in the restrooms. This bar is a simulation of an abandoned manufacturing facility that has been converted to a lively brewery. A simulation of a fulfilled emptiness; a flaw that found its fetish. In the porn terms from before, this is the version of the story where fetish sex is acceptable and safe. It is normal. Whatever the motivation behind this brewpub, the warehouse aesthetic is spreading, yet ambiguous and unclaimed. There is something in the Rust Belt that isn't entirely reproducible, yet a new building can get close enough for most to desire and enjoy it. That is a successful branding recipe.

As displayed by ruin porn photography, empty structures also entice the imagination to consider what it would fill that structure with. Porn directors do so in truly creative ways, but I'll leave that up to your imagination. This leads us to an interesting conclusion: an old warehouse is a desirable backdrop because it is cute, much in the same way a kitten or a baby is cute because we want to hold, feed, and care for it. Cute defines the ability of capital to exploit our maternal instinct. Interestingly enough, Rust Belt warehouses aren't exactly flying off of the shelves. In fact, Cleveland is lagging behind. Maybe it's the weather, but maybe it's just a confidence issue.

Architecture is at its best when it is indiscernible from fantasy. Digital media and culture cause physical place to mean less and less, making the aesthetic and experiential affordances of a place increasingly valuable. As hegemonic barriers of sexuality fall, the fetish sites of old become important history.

This is an architectural call to arms. What Cleveland needs is not discovering some lost authenticity but encouraging others to seek a simulation of what is thought of as authenticity. We need to convert empty warehouses, yes, but also, new construction must find a way to be a little less straight and a little more kinky, in both senses of the word. We need brick that is a little crumbled, beams and columns that twist and turn, and pieces of leftover machinery with a curious presence. What would happen to Cleveland if suddenly a lot more people were asking themselves, "What could I do with a big empty warehouse?"

# Ghosts of Bay View

## KEN GERMANSON

from **The Milwaukee Anthology**

Howard Zinn had a shameful confession to make in Bay View in the late 1990s.

Zinn, author of *A People's History of the United States* and one of the most informed historians on US working-class history, was in our Milwaukee neighborhood to join an annual commemoration of Wisconsin's largest labor massacre. At that year's event, Zinn said it was the first time he had really heard about those who organized—and died—in the 1886 Bay View Rolling Mills tragedy.

It's a good bet, then, that the bloody events, and even the standing state historical marker, have been lost over the years on many of the customers at the nearby popular restaurants and pubs in this increasingly hip neighborhood, to say nothing of the thousands of people who drive past daily on to work, into downtown.

As obscure as the meaning of the site might be for some, on the first Sunday of May for the past thirty-two years, it becomes a lively and important historical reminder for several hundred unionists, neighborhood residents, history buffs, activists, and just plain curious citizens. The event has grown from historical commemoration to one that features a reenactment with twelve-foot-tall puppets and volunteer actors wearing the gray outfits of nineteenth-century workers, followed up with stirring speeches and inspirational singing.

In 2018—the 132nd Anniversary Commemoration of the Bay View Tragedy—some three hundred crowded onto the cramped site, mostly standing, greeting each other like the long friends and colleagues they are but often realizing the last time they saw each other was likely at this same event a year earlier. Shortly before the program begins, a group of several dozen march up—many wearing the pink hardhats of the "Women of Steel," a steelworkers union group—having completed a short march that roughly follows the events of May 5, 1886.

This annual ceremony is held to pay homage to seven who gave their lives in the historic quest to establish the eight-hour workday. The Bay View neighborhood event, sponsored by the Wisconsin Labor History Society, serves as a reminder of those who died, shot down by the state militia while in a march of some 1,500 workers on May 5, 1886, toward the giant Bay View Rolling Mills plant on the shore of Lake Michigan, in what would become Wisconsin's bloodiest labor incident.

"While we want to remember their deaths, we need to celebrate their courage," said John Schneider, prominent Milwaukee actor and director, who narrated a reenactment of the 1886 incident. "Their deaths were not in vain. They won; the movement won."

Within ten months of the massacre, the workers' People's Party took over the Milwaukee City Council. Many of those who marched in 1886 went on to create the Socialist Party that, by the early 1900s, teamed up with "Fighting Bob" La Follette and his Progressive Republicans to make Wisconsin a forerunner in pro-worker and good government legislation. Socialist leadership in the city led to making Milwaukee one of the nation's most egalitarian of cities, as well as one of the best-run cities, a claim made in a 1935 *Time* magazine cover story about Socialist Mayor Dan Hoan.

It can seem like distant history, at times. In 2011, Republican Governor Scott Walker infamously stripped a majority of the state's public-sector unions of collective bargaining power, under protests that shut down the state capitol. And, 132 years since the Bay View massacre, the eight-hour workday is still an issue, Milwaukee Area Labor Council President Pam Fendt reminded the audience.

"How many of us work more than forty hours a week and still bring work home?" she asked, singling out teachers and nurses. (It wasn't until 1938 that the Federal Wage and House Law was passed that created the forty-hour workweek, though never explicitly an eight-hour day.)

Fendt quoted a *New York Times* article that said many are working sixty hours a week; she cited the galling pay disparity between CEOs and the average worker. Fendt urged the labor movement to redouble efforts to bring change, particularly through organizing.

"I see hope out there," she said. "I see leaders who want to make Milwaukee again a great union town."

Picking up the organizing theme, Kristin Fecteau, an apprentice electrician and member of IBEW Local 494, said every member must be an organizer, taking every chance to engage coworkers, friends, neighbors, and others in discussions about unions. This is an important way in which to combat negative beliefs about unions, she said. Unionists can't be complacent, she said, calling attention to a union election that was lost by a few votes because many members failed to show up to cast ballots.

Her comments ended on a stirring plea: "Be proud. Be committed. Be productive and be union!"

This year's program was emceed by Anita Zeidler, a UW-Milwaukee retiree and a member of the American Federation of Teachers, whose role in many past commemorations involved laying a memorial wreath at the foot of the state historical mark at the site of the event. Her late father, Frank, was Socialist mayor of Milwaukee from 1948 to 1960. (Frank Zeidler was part of the event's planning committee and a regular event speaker from its founding in 1986 to his death in 2006.)

Barbara Leigh, former director of the Milwaukee Public Theatre, joined in direction by Schneider, produced the dramatic reenactment of the march and the shooting, a staple since 2011. Popular Milwaukee drummer Jahmés Finlayson provided accompaniment while Craig Siemsen, retired Milwaukee Public Schools teacher and union member, led the crowd in traditional sing-a-longs of "Ghosts of Bay View" and "Solidarity Forever." (The late Milwaukee folksinger Larry Penn composed "Ghosts of Bay View," and it has been sung at every event since 1986.)

History tells us repeatedly that oppressed people need to come together in solidarity to seek positive change. Whether it was in the winter of 1936–37, when autoworkers in Flint, Michigan, sat down on the job, setting off successful union organizing in the factories across America; or in 1955, when Rosa Parks refused to sit in the rear of the bus in Montgomery, Alabama, igniting the civil rights movement that was to bring momentous legislation a decade later; or in 1969, when gay rights activists stood up against police at the Stonewall Tavern, giving birth to the gay rights movement that eventually brought greater protections for the LGBTQ community.

To many, the 1886 Bay View Tragedy was a "loss" for the cause of workers. Coming one day after Chicago's Haymarket Affair, in which nine lost their lives, the two events were described in the newspapers as riots composed of thugs and anarchists, a characterization that tolled a temporary death knell to the nationwide campaign for an eight-hour workday.

Common to these worker and citizen revolts is the fact that, at the time, they were all "unpopular" in the public media and among the establishment. The Bay View marchers were called "rioters" and "thugs," even though they were mainly foundry and factory workers merely seeking a better life. Most were Polish, and their lives were hardly valued with the establishment or the newspapers of the day; sounds similar to today's treatment of Hispanics and African Americans. Note also that virtually all those in the other solidarity movements of the last 150 years were called rioters, terrorists, anarchists, or "Commies."

All of this is understood by the few hundred people who show up each year at the Bay View Rolling Mills historic marker site. They're reminded that in the fight for justice, there are often losses and sacrifices, but that if the oppressed continue to act in solidarity and perseverance, success will come.

That's why, amidst the somber atmosphere in 2018, as we relived the grim history of May 5, 1886, through tears shed during the reading of the names of the seven victims, there is an obvious stirring of hope rising among the audience that comes from greeting old and new friends and allies in the struggle.

There have been no polls taken to show why hundreds show up each year. But my guess is that dedicated kindred spirits believe solidarity is still alive and that it's time to dedicate themselves to the eternal fight for justice, at the workplace and in the community as a whole.

# Something Like Irresponsibility

### HARMONY COX

**from Sweeter Voices Still: An LGBTQ Anthology from Middle America**

In the months before I came out of the closet and asked my husband for a separation, I did a lot of things. I googled terms like "later-in-life lesbian" and "irreconcilable differences." I quietly began the work of separating our finances. I slept in my bed—my newly purchased separate bed, where I'd been sleeping while we tried to work things out—felt the cold space next to me, and cried.

But mostly, I drove.

Ohio is my home state, the place where I have lived most of my life. I suspect there might be something uniquely Ohioan about being soothed by the highway.

In 1984, the year I was born, the Ohio Division of Transit and Tourism came up with a new slogan to explain our state to the rest of the country: "Ohio, The Heart of It All"—ostensibly because Ohio is kind of shaped like a heart, if you squint at a map of the United States and don't know much about anatomy. And thus, if Ohio is the heart of it all, the chambers are made by the vascular divisions of its interstates. Vehicles are the blood cells of Ohio, carrying people to their intended destinations swiftly and safely. To occupy one of these cells, to be in transit, is one of my favorite things to do.

Every distance in Ohio is not measured in feet or miles but minutes spent driving to your destination. If you hop on I-71, you can drive Ohio's tip to tail in just about six hours. I-70 will take you east to west, Indiana to West Virginia, in about the same amount of time. My favorite, I-270, is known as the Outerbelt. It takes you on a neat, never-ending circular tour of Columbus and its many suburbs. I live on the city side, where the curves glide you past the tiny, glittering skyscrapers of our old-fashioned downtown.

———————

Driving these highways is a practical way to get around, but it's also a way to get your head straight. I would make up some excuse to get myself out of the house and spend hours in the darkness, circling Columbus with a pack of cigarettes and a massive Sonic lemonade. I'd lose myself in the meditative hum of wheels on asphalt, counting the numbers on the exits and letting the high-beams distract me from my tears.

I'd been through three therapists in ten years, each of whom had their own exit on this highway. The Lane Avenue exit led to the university hospital, where I'd gone in graduate school to see a therapist for help in sorting out my pre-wedding anxieties. He listened patiently for twenty minutes, then he told me I had to call it off because he'd never known a queer woman to stay happily married to a straight man. I didn't have the courage to question him, so I let myself believe my growing discomfort with my impending matrimony was my own fault, because I was too queer to be a good wife. So I put my queerness aside and refused to think about it for a long time.

Another exit, this one to Granville. Where I sought out therapy again, this time when a close relationship with a friend became confusing. She had found a new boyfriend, and I was experiencing a sharp and painful jealousy that I didn't have the context to understand.

(But the highway does; there, the exit that leads to the favorite restaurant where she held my hand and told me I was the most important person in her world. There, the exit to the bus station where she wept as she kissed me goodbye! The only thing she needed more than me was to stay in her comfort zone, so you can guess why we parted ways in the end.)

After I described my plight, my new therapist leaned forward with a confused look on his face.

"But if you think you're bisexual, how do you know if you're in love with a friend or you just care about them a lot?"

I stared at him, biting back the sting of tears. "I don't know. That's why I'm seeing you."

It was the third therapist, off the exit to Upper Arlington, who actually understood. She was a specialist in LGBTQ identity issues, and she helped me untangle my confusion and jealousy and set me on the right path. She forced me to acknowledge the truth—that I was a closeted queer woman, that I was deeply unhappy as a result, and that as much as I loved my husband, I could not be the wife he needed me to be. That was when I realized I would have to eventually set out alone, away from the man who I thought I'd be spending the rest of my life with. This journey, like my endless looping trips on the highway, could only be my own.

Realizing it was one thing. Accepting it was something else entirely.

I had already been testing our boundaries, but I didn't cheat on him. We even had a grudgingly open relationship toward the end, when we were trying to figure out if we could possibly stay together. It didn't matter. I knew he resented me for it, and I still felt unfaithful to him. I was the one who was going out by myself to flirt with women. I never actively courted their attention, but I never did anything to dissuade them when they clocked me and complimented my leather jackets and bought me drinks.

I never went home with them either; I'd always make some excuse, an early day at work or feeling a bit under the weather, and I'd leave before they'd think to ask for my number. Just a few minutes spent on vacation from my straight life, then back in the car. It is an easy jump from the brewery district to the highway interchange. I would be back on the road before I realized what I was driving away from. However, I never went home, not right away.

Instead, I drove.

As I drove, I'd feel my body drift with the curve of the highway, my head gently bobbing from left to right. I'd count off the exits to the suburbs. The Easton condos. Westerville. Hilliard, and beyond that, Gahanna. These were the places that had sprawled into clusters of McMansions during the Columbus population boom of the mid-2000s. Acres of forests and farmlands, obliterated and replaced with cheesy-sounding gated communities meant to honor the things that had been sacrificed to create them. The Ravine at Scioto. Farmer's Street. The Residency at Creekside.

The prevalence of gigantic single-family homes in Columbus is both environmentally irresponsible and morally obscene; it's the definition of sprawl and waste. But developers built these places because in my town, there is a thirst for this American dream. Sometimes it seems like everyone I know is moving out of the city, away from the bustle and fun of happy hours and into the "starter houses" that will shelter the families they're ready to bring into being. The toy doll pairings of my coupled friends, taking the next step.

When I drove by these exits, I would think of the people who lived there. People I knew, people who were also married, people who embraced a fate that seemed worse than death to me. I'd imagine these people seated at the Target tables in their IKEA kitchens, sorted neatly into houses with the exact same floor plan, each house's vinyl siding a complementary shade of pale pink or blue. Happy with the life they'd chosen.

I would cry and ask myself what was wrong with me, what was broken in me that made me want something else. Why imagining leaving my metro lifestyle behind for the sake of a school district made me want to drive my car off the side of the road and into a telephone pole. I'd try to picture myself with a baby in my arms, a man by my side, but all I could see was static.

————

When I got tired of listening to myself cry, I'd turn on the radio. Singing along with a car stereo is the cheapest and most readily available form of therapy that midwesterners are willing to accept. People might think it odd if you sit in a small room with a stranger and try to draw lines between your ugly past and your current neuroses, but nobody will look twice if you spend a few minutes howling along to Journey's greatest hits while stuck in the I-161 traffic circle clusterfuck.

My favorite band to listen to during these late-night drives was Against Me!, a punk band I'd kind of liked in high school but rediscovered with a vengeance during this time of woe. There was one particular song that I liked to sing along with: "Pretty Girls (The Mover)," off of the album *Searching for a Former Clarity*. It's a song written by Laura Jane Grace about the pieces of herself that ended relationships with women before they could begin, and her fear that nobody (including herself) can accept her for who she really is:

> And if she says yes, know what intentions might be
> If one thing leads to another and there's some chemistry
> You cannot lie, you have to tell the truth
> You have to explain why this could never be
> Cause there are things that cannot be undone
> There are mistakes that will never be forgiven
> Sometimes at night, I pray to wake
> A different person in a different place
> I just want to be young, I want to live
> God, I want to be healthy, I don't want this problem
> You wouldn't think something like irresponsibility
> Would complicate something like asking for some company

But there are things you must accept as said and done
There are truths you must learn to confront
You can pray all night and day
You'll always wake the same person in the same place

It's a sad and anxious song, and I felt it in my bones every time it came on. I'd sing aloud with it loudly, freely weeping, taking comfort in the misery I shared with Grace. Sometimes I would put it on repeat and let it loop around me the same way I endlessly looped around my city in the night.

One night, I accidently put on the live recording of the song instead of the studio version. I was surprised to learn that the lyrics had changed since it was first recorded. When *Searching for a Former Clarity* was released, Laura Jane Grace had not come out as transgender yet. She was still grappling with that realization and what it meant for her, and she wasn't ready to share it. So she'd selectively censored some of the lyrics to the songs she wrote about it. In this particular song, she'd used "irresponsibility" instead of "gender identity" for the studio recording. The live recording gave it the context and meaning it was intended to have.

The true meaning of the song hit me like a slap. Of course, the song was about being closeted and the way it isolates you from other people. No wonder I felt so connected to it, even before I knew what it was about. I don't mean to conflate my journey with that of Grace's, or borrow the pain of transgender individuals to make a point about my own sexuality. But the ache of hiding yourself from the world for so long, and the grinding pain of working so hard to avoid your own truth, is a theme that could not help but resonate with me in that moment. It felt like the song had come to me before I'd realized how much I needed it, in a disguise so I'd receive the message without overthinking it. Only now did I understand what the lyrics really meant, and why they made me sob into my lemonade.

As Grace wisely notes, there are truths you must learn to confront. A punk song may not be the ideal cardinal north for a journey into a new world, but I could not deny that hiding who I was and what I wanted was crushing me, and that sustaining a marriage on the back of my pain wasn't going to work forever. I had to stop running from the truth. No matter how much therapy I underwent, no matter how I prayed or pleaded for something else, I would always be the same person at the end of the day. And that person didn't want to be married, and wasn't particularly attracted to cisgender men, and had never let herself live openly as a queer person before. There was a whole new future before me, so much unexplored possibility if I just stopped driving in the same circles and let myself consider a different path. I deserved to be happy in a way the exits to the suburbs never could provide. I was always meant to keep moving.

So I told my husband the truth. We recognized our differences were irreconcilable, and we split up. I remained in my hometown, determined to chase my own happiness until I found it. All I had to do was end my marriage of a decade, come out to my friends and family, and learn how to be queer at the tender young age of thirty-five. Not an easy journey to start, but at least I was finally ready to begin.

# All Sales Final

## SHARON BLOYD-PESHKIN

### from **Rust Belt Chicago**

It's a cold, gray, blustery March morning on Chicago's near North Side. Taxis, delivery trucks, and luxury vehicles swoosh along Grand Avenue and Orleans Street, kicking up road salt, honking and jockeying for space as they pass condo buildings, self-storage facilities, coffee shops, and investment firms.

River North, promoted by the city as "the go-to district for those who appreciate fine art and design," has undergone an almost complete transformation in the past four decades, from a place of manufacturing to a locus of consumption. Long gone are most of the factories and the blue-collar workers who once gave this part of the City of Big Shoulders its brawn; in their stead, the neighborhood now warehouses workers of a white-collar sort, and the shops, restaurants, bars, and services that supply their more patrician needs.

But in the shadow of the new construction, an older, three-story building remains: Clark & Barlow Hardware, a business that served Chicago's construction, manufacturing, and railroad industries for more than a century. It's a hardware store where men in Carhartts who actually wear them to work line up at the counter to request tools and parts that aren't stocked by the Ace Hardware down the street or the Home Depot across town; a place when the salespeople swiftly turn to the shelves behind them and extract those obscure items; a place where many employees have worked for their entire adult lives because, they say, they feel like a family.

A place that is closing.

**LIQUIDATING TO THE BARE WALLS**

**Sale ends soon**

The signs outside are unmistakable, from the banners flapping in the wind to the trucks pulling up at the loading dock to cart away deeply discounted merchandise. In the front hallway, the steel shelves are for sale, $25 per section. The hard hats are $5 each, final. Interested in the wood display cabinets? Make an offer.

Angela Mucci, sixty-four, sits in the first-floor office, processing some of the markdowns. She's worked at Clark & Barlow for more than half her life, starting at the downtown location, 123 West Lake Street, which was displaced in 1980 by the soon-to-be-built State of Illinois Center (later renamed the James R. Thompson Center). She fondly recalls the variety of tasks she performed there, from patching together phone calls on the second-floor switchboard to sending customers their change and receipts in metal cups that sped along an overhead wire. A frame containing two black-and-white photographs of the Lake Street location hangs above her desk.

But she's rarely at her desk—one of the reasons she has worked here so long. Rather, the soon-to-be-grandmother spends her work hours sending invoices, ordering out-of-stock items, and pushing carts and even brooms. "I don't want to sit in an office," she says. "I want to work like this."

The other reason is the people, she says, starting with Joseph J. Sullivan, who owned Clark & Barlow for forty-six years until his death in 2010. "It was a good place to work, and he was a good boss," Mucci says, pointing to Sullivan's photo on the wall. "It was a place that you really wanted to stay. It was like family."

In fact, for many people, it really was family. Two of Sullivan's six children, Teri and Judy, worked at Clark & Barlow for decades. Mucci applied for a job because her sister, Sophie, worked at Clark & Barlow. Sophie met her husband, Marty, there. Many employees worked alongside their siblings and cousins. People stayed until they retired, and sometimes until they died.

Now, long-time employees who once worked together to stock the shelves are endeavoring to empty them. "It was a great work environment," says Michelle Diaz, forty-five, who began at Clark & Barlow in 1991 and is now a manager.

Diaz, whose mother, sister, daughter, and cousin followed her to Clark & Barlow, is one of six remaining employees, down from twenty-three when the building and company were sold in 2012, and more than fifty when she started working here. She recalls her first boss, John Patdu, who came from the Philippines in 1972 when he was twenty-four years old. Patdu walked into the Lake Street location and saw "a bunch of old guys working there," Diaz says, but he applied for a job anyway and was hired in accounts payable. Patdu stayed for forty years. "Clark & Barlow was my first job and my last job," says Patdu, now sixty-eight, who retired after Joe Sullivan died.

The *Chicago Tribune* obituaries tell similar stories. There's Herbert Christiansen, who worked for Clark & Barlow for seventy-one years until his retirement at age ninety; and Harold Schroeder, who began as a stock clerk right out of high school, became a buyer, and retired at age sixty-five. They and other former colleagues are fondly remembered by the employees who remain during these final days.

**Check it out.**

**70% OFF BOX PRICE**

**ALL SALES FINAL**

"I've only been here fifteen years," says Don Schelberger, sixty-two, who works behind the counter. It took him about a year to figure out where everything was stashed on the shelves, but now, when a customer requests an item, no matter how unusual, "I can go any place in the building and know where it's at."

Over the past decade, he's watched the clientele change. At first, most customers were contractors, railroad laborers, and construction workers. Then the people who lived in the newly built condos started coming in. But the main client base remained those in the building trades.

"Hey, Dan. What time do you leave in the morning?" he asks Dan Mogan, who commutes in from the south suburbs before the store opens at 6:00 a.m.

"Five," replies Mogan, who has worked for Clark & Barlow for thirty-three years. "There's always someone outside waiting to buy something."

Mogan, too, applied for a job because his brother worked there. "I didn't know much about hardware," he admits. But after stints on the dock, at will call, and in shipping, he learned where everything was squirreled away and started working behind the counter.

The counter at Clark & Barlow was the front line for finding all manner of uncommon hardware. "There is no other place you can go and say, 'I need this screw,' and they know exactly where it is and will sell you one of them," Diaz says, pantomiming a customer holding up a singular object. "We were still one-on-one. We were more personal. We were known for our customer service."

Now, customers poke around areas that previously were restricted to employees like Schelberger and Mogan. "It's strange watching people wandering through," Diaz says. They paw through the shelves, brush dust off old boxes, squint at unfamiliar parts. They ask whether they can still get a particular tape or tool or trowel. "We've been pulling things out that've been buried for the past twenty years," Schelberger says.

Sheldon Holden, fifty-five, an airport baggage handler who lives in Chicago, came in when he saw the signs outside. "I drove past here a week ago and I thought they were just having a big-time sale," he says. "Then I looked at the signs real good and thought, 'Wait a minute; they're going out of business.'"

Holden recalls visiting Clark & Barlow with his father when he was a child and becoming a regular customer when, as an adult, he owned an older home. "If you had something in your house that dated back to the forties, fifties, sixties, you could probably go in there and get something to replace it. You can't do that at Home Depot," he says. He also came in for advice. "If you was tackling a project you thought was hard, after you talked to them, it turned out it was simple."

"I'm going to miss the service," Holden says. "This was the Rolls-Royce of hardware stores. It was the last of the Mohicans."

That kind of customer satisfaction is what made working at Clark & Barlow attractive to Teri Sullivan, one of the owner's daughters, who worked for a car rental company before taking a job at the store in the mid-1990s. "The hard-to-find things, oh yeah, they'd come in and say, 'I was told you have everything,'" she says of the store's customers. "We totally cared about them and took it personally when they needed things and went out of our way to find them."

But the bread and butter of the business were contractors and construction workers. "I would say our business was 80 percent with contractors and 20 percent retail," says Patdu, who worked as Clark & Barlow's comptroller from 1975 until 2012.

Now, construction trucks and vans are at the loading dock, and men in sweatshirts and work gloves who don't want to talk to reporters are hauling away what they can salvage. A group of Amish men from Ontario, Wisconsin, who stand out in their white shirts and brimmed hats, drive away with a load of axe and scythe handles along with miscellaneous hand tools and hardware.

"I know for a fact there's nothing like [Clark & Barlow] in the city," Teri Sullivan says. "They're going to have to go to a Home Depot, where they're not going to find those things, or online. They're not going to be able to go in and ask a person who can help."

"All the contractors are like, 'Oh my God. Where are we going to go?'" Mucci says.

**$10 each**
**SOLD**

**Watch Your Step**
**Sale/Sale/Sale**

Upstairs, past the hot pink and fluorescent green posters partially obscuring the neon "Decorative Hardware Showroom" sign, the dim lighting and the soft sound of an AM radio station create the atmosphere of a theater set. Track lighting illuminates a room full of boxes, most open and exposing sinks and toilets. A few bathtubs rest near the doorway, and some mirrors lean against the wall. You almost expect Willy Loman to come in and offer to sell you a bidet.

Judy Sullivan, another of Joe Sullivan's daughters, worked in the showroom for more than two decades. "We had everything, and if we didn't have it, we would get it," she recalls. Those were the days before the inventory was in computer databases, when sales were written up on paper and stored away in file cabinets. She left in 2012, about the time that Studio 41, a home design retailer of kitchen and bath fixtures, hardware, and cabinetry, purchased the business.

Across the hall is another room where floor-to-ceiling industrial shelves are crowded with lock sets, hinges, and cylinders. A poster of Miss Makita 2002, Amber Goetz, holding a drill, covers the side of a filing cabinet; a 1992 calendar with a tool-wielding blonde in a pink bikini is taped to a pole. A man in a backpack shuffles shelf to shelf, removes a lock set from its box, leaves both on separate shelves. The wind rattles the steel-frame windows.

The main offices inhabited a room full of beige metal cubicles, now deserted, where phone lists are still tacked above empty phone jacks. A few old IBM terminals remain, along with blank white boards and metal filing cabinets. A sheriff paid for the enormous safe but hasn't yet come back to retrieve it. The lady who purchased the coffin carrier also needs to return for it before the building closes for good.

The basement, once off-limits, contains some of the oddest items: railroad car lifters, crane winches, scythe handles. A display board full of casters suggests the full cycle Clark & Barlow has been through over the past half century.

**$5 each. Final.**
**All hinges $5 set**
**Pulls & Plates $10 each**

The caster business is where Joe Sullivan got his start. He and his older brother, Harry, worked for Payson Manufacturing, selling industrial-grade casters. One of Sullivan's clients was Jack Barlow, co-owner of Clark & Barlow since 1923.

"After he worked for Payson for five or six years, he went to Mr. Barlow, who was old, and says, 'I respect you. I know that someday I want to run my own business. If one of your friends ever wants to get out of whatever business they're in, I'd be interested in talking to them,'" recalls Joe Sullivan Jr., his oldest son. "So two years later, Mr. Barlow says, 'What do you think of this business?'"

According to Joe Sullivan Jr. and all four of his sisters, what followed was a combination of savvy bargaining and gentlemanly behavior. The accounts differ in some of the particulars, but they agree that Sullivan got wind that someone else was interested and quickly consummated the deal, at which point the two shook hands. Then another offer was made—perhaps by Barlow's sons-in-law, perhaps by someone else—for more money. But in the end, Joe recalls, "My dad says, 'You shook my hand.' And Barlow says, 'You know, you're right. I did shake your hand; we've got a deal.'"

By all accounts, Clark & Barlow thrived under Sullivan's ownership. It expanded from one to four locations; Sullivan's family of eight moved from a three-bedroom house to a six-bedroom house. Sullivan was beloved by his employees in part because he didn't interfere too much with the daily operations of the business. Instead, he was out making connections and sealing deals, as well as pursuing his own eclectic interests, which included playing golf, racing horses, and singing in local bars. "My dad didn't live to work at all," Joe Sullivan Jr. says. "He said, 'This is great. I don't want to grow the business anymore. I'm very comfortable.' So it's not the American dream of dominating the Chicago area."

But while Sullivan hewed to Barlow's vision—stocking the shelves with everything anyone could possibly need, prioritizing hands-on customer service over computerization and cost-cutting—things changed around Clark & Barlow. Discount, big-box hardware stores moved into the neighborhood; the internet provided information about and access to hard-to-find items; competition among online retailers led to quick and cheap delivery. Business began to drop off. Clark & Barlow closed the other locations, but even in River North, revenue dwindled. At its peak, Joe Sullivan Jr. estimates Clark & Barlow did $10 million in sales. By 2015, it was down to a quarter of that. And meanwhile, costs were skyrocketing. Real estate taxes alone were $80,000. "Clark & Barlow, they're not here anymore because they didn't change. My dad didn't change," he says. "They continued to do business the old-fashioned way, and ultimately that led to their demise."

After Joe Sullivan Sr. died, his children looked at the books. Again, accounts differ a bit, but they sold the building and the land to Onni Group for $8.8 million, and the business to Studio 41 for an undisclosed amount that is rumored to have been very low. Joe Sullivan Jr. took care of the handshake on this transaction, but it was far more formal. In exchange for purchasing the business, Studio 41 agreed to offer every Clark & Barlow employee a job and take care of emptying out decades of inventory from the building. "I look at Studio 41 as, they saved us," Joe Sullivan Jr. says. "Studio 41 did Clark & Barlow a favor, and Clark & Barlow did Studio 41 a favor because of the name, the history, etc."

"It was sentimental. It was a little heartbreaking to see it go," says his sister, Amy Schroeder.

**Make an offer**
**SOLD!**

After Studio 41 purchased the business, most of the employees stayed on until the building was emptied. Only Michelle Diaz and two other Clark & Barlow employees accepted the offer to continue on working for Studio 41.

After that, the great sell-off began. Prices were steadily reduced; spaces were gradually cleared. Eventually, the cleaning service was discontinued and the employees had to clean the bathrooms and sweep the floors themselves.

"I think the last day is going to be the hardest because it's an era that's ending, and who knows what's really going to happen?" says Diaz.

Most of the long-timers have decided they don't want to find out. "I think I'm just going to call it a day," Schelberger says. "That's enough. It's hard."

Mucci, too, chose not to take a job at Studio 41. "I have my good memories, so that's it," she says. "When Mr. Sullivan passed away, to me, the store passed away.'"

On a dreary March afternoon, this is how it ends, slowly, bit by bit, bolt by bolt, as the wind blows leaves around the dumpster outside.

# The Human Toll of the Steel Mill

## JOSEPH S. PETE

from **The Gary Anthology**

You can't fully appreciate the sheer scope of the hulking rust-dappled Gary Works steel mill unless you've passed through the gates.

US Steel's flagship steel mill, the whole initial reason for Gary's existence, looms over the city at the terminus of the main road, Broadway, sprawling across seven miles of Lake Michigan lakefront like an industrial colossus bestride a once-pristine natural world it's subjugated and befouled, supplanting sand dunes and scrub oaks. City Hall was built right across the street from the behemoth integrated mill—of the type that's so massive and capital-intensive no new ones have been built in the United States since the 1960s—at 1 North Broadway in the company town as an intentional gesture to remind future mayors who was really in charge.

But Gary Works has become an increasingly walled-off and isolated fortress from the city it spawned. Multiple railroad tracks, the interurban South Shore Line, the Indiana Toll Road, and the moat of the Grand Calumet River physically separate it from the downtown and the rest of the city. The crest of the faded robin egg blue No. 1 BOP Shop barely peeks out amid a thicket of high-tension power lines and a miasma of steam rolling up off the mill like spray off waves on Lake Michigan. The formidable mill, which helped raise skyscrapers, span bridges, and keep countless cars rolling off the assembly line during the twentieth century has been hollowed out by automation, the ravages of foreign steel dumping, and general industrial decline that's scarred much of the Midwest. The *Chicago Tribune* reported it lost $1 million a day during part of the 1980s, and executives even discussed shutting it down.

Today, it employs a few thousand workers, a far cry from the thirty thousand mostly immigrant or transplant steelworkers who clocked in there during its heyday, earning comfortable middle-class wages hard-won in negotiations by the United Steelworkers union. The decline has been stark: the mill now employs about half as many people as it did during the 1990s. Many of the workers no longer live in the city, instead commuting in from the suburbs of south Lake County or Porter County to the east. The merchant bar mills that helped build Chicago's skyscrapers and many other buildings have long been dormant, rendered obsolete by mini-mills. Twelve blast furnaces once blazed at Gary Works; today, only four remain, and one was idled because of slumping steel prices in the summer of 2019. The mill once operated 838 coke ovens; today, zero remain. As its operations on the lakeshore have shrunk, the Pittsburgh-based company is no longer as involved in the community as it once was long ago, no longer sending a choir around town to sing Christmas carols, organizing intramural sports leagues for its employees, or sponsoring various causes around town. It no longer even has any ads on the outfield wall at its namesake US Steel Yard, where the independent, minor league Gary SouthShore RailCats play.

You have to enter the mill to really appreciate the inhuman scope, the impossible size of the place. The rusting buildings loom so large they make Ford F-150s look like Hot Wheels. You could walk through hulking finishing lines, where steel coil whizzes by for nearly a mile without seeing a single hard-hatted soul, such as at the five-story continuous casters where the only workers monitor computer screens. The mill can feel as cavernous as a skyscraper-lined street in the downtown of a major city and as vast as the windswept dunes that ring much of Lake Michigan's southern shore. The heat from a blast furnace or super-heated metal at a hot strip mill is so palpable it can physically knock you back. Step close enough and the wave of heat will make you wince, grind your teeth, and stagger away.

You have to work at the mill to appreciate how dangerous it truly is.

Every day, steelworkers toil by volcanic heat and moving machinery that can weigh thousands of pounds. Steelworker is the sixth most dangerous job in the United States, with 29.8 deaths per one hundred thousand residents, according to the US Occupational Safety and Health Administration. Steelworkers can get crushed, burned, or electrocuted. They can get hit by trains, pinned under forklifts, or fall from great heights. For all the platitudes they preach after safety being job number one, no amount of steel being worth a single human life, and the importance of everyone returning home at the end of a shift, if you get killed at a steel mill, it's almost certain to be closed casket. The human toll is apparent if you visit any union hall in the Gary area: they all have memorial walls inscribed with the names of the dead, steelworkers killed on the job. I've seen the toll firsthand at local

Worker's Memorial Day ceremonies, where surviving family members lay wreaths, their tear-stained faces contorted with grief.

As the steel industry and labor reporter for the *Times of Northwest Indiana* newspaper, I've had to cover a number of tragic deaths and fatal workplace accidents at local steel mills. One night, on a sweat-stained bedsheet that needed washing, long after I had left the newsroom for the day, I sprawled out, ready to sleep, when my phone started buzzing with tips. It rumbled on the cheap, dingy mattress like Godzilla stomping across the countryside. Steelworkers texted and DMed, demanding a report about a fatal accident at Gary Works, the granddaddy and gold standard of Region steel mills in the heavily industrialized corner of Chicagoland that's now home to half the country's blast furnace capacity. Built in 1906 after wild horses tamed the wild dunes of the Lake Michigan shoreline, Gary started out as a company town to house workers who walked or took streetcars to the mill. Gary Works was the world's largest steel mill erected by the world's first billion-dollar corporation that was once the world's largest steelmaker, and the enterprise has taken its toll on Gary in wear and tear on bodies, in pollution of the lake, air, and soil, and in the slow-motion economic debacle of a company town anchor that's slowly withering away, a fading institution that's failed the town built to serve it. And Gary Works has taken its toll in blood.

It was after midnight in September 2016 when I first learned of the death of Jonathan Arrizola, an electrician from the nearby suburb of Valparaiso, who left behind a family and kids. I started frantically emailing the Lake County coroner, company spokespeople, and union officials, anyone I could think of. Though I didn't expect to hear anything back so soon so late, the story possessed a sense of urgency and quickly began to come together: The thirty-year-old maintenance worker and married father of two was killed while working on a four-man crew tasked with troubleshooting a crane in the US Steel slab storage yard in the largest steel mill in North America late the night before. He was a Navy veteran who had been deployed on a humanitarian mission to Pakistan but was killed after returning home to the United States, where he was supposed to be safe. A widely circulated photo after his death showed him relaxing shirtless at the beach, his children by his side, the sun at his back, his whole future splayed out before him.

For the union, Arrizola's death was dreaded, feared, even expected. "As terrible as it sounds, haven't we been saying that something was coming?" then USW Local 1014 President Rodney Lewis said at the time. Union officials had been warning of safety risks for some time as a result of US Steel's Carnegie Way cost-cutting initiative and the consultant McKinsey & Co.'s layoffs and demotions of maintenance workers. The union warned the cuts put workers at risk by shutting down safety training and putting off preventative maintenance, causing work orders to pile up and forcing steelworkers into roving bare-bones crews to do maintenance in the areas of the sprawling mill—itself bigger than some small towns—they are unfamiliar with. It even appeals the bloodletting to a third-party arbiter, arguing it was a contract violation that threatened workers' safety and well-being.

His wife said he had explicitly warned her things were getting more dangerous at the mill and that he had suffered an electric shock in a separate accident the week before his death. "He was constantly complaining about the McKinsey group cutting back workers," his widow, Whitney Arrizola, told the *Times of Northwest Indiana* at the time. "There was always some kind of close call with someone he worked with. I never imagined that something would happen to Jon, he was always the safest guy I knew." Her husband, the kind of guy who paid for the dinner of a service member he didn't know at El Salto, left behind an eight-year-old son and a four-year-old who was about to celebrate his birthday. "All they care about is making money," Whitney Arrizola said at the time. "They don't care that it affects other people. He has a four-year-old who's turning five. They keep cutting when they should have a safer environment for people. It shouldn't be all about the money. I have no husband now, my children have no father. I have no idea how I'm going to pay for my house or my car, any of our bills, I was a stay-at-home mother. I have no experiences, Jon was everything to me." The company cut off her family's health insurance almost right away, but concerned colleagues and well-wishers raised $14,000 on GoFundMe to cover expenses.

Arrizola and the sixty-seven-year-old maintenance technician Charles Kremke both died of accidental electrocution at the understaffed mill in 2016. The state fined the steelmaker a total of $42,000 for their deaths after inspectors found a number of serious safety violations at Gary Works, a tiny pittance for a company that pulled in a profit of $1.1 billion in 2018. After their deaths and union protests outside the mill gates in downtown Gary, US Steel eventually restored the staffing levels and stopped the practice of putting roving short-handed labor gangs in unfamiliar places. The Carnegie Way cost-cutting initiative ended, and the CEO who pushed it got kicked to the curb once steel prices rebounded and all the austerity started to cost the company money.

But Gary Works and other steel mills remain extremely dangerous places to earn a living. No matter how much the union presses for safety, no matter how much the company pays lip service to it and "employees being its most valuable asset," there are just inherent hazards, like steel coils weighed by the ton and blast furnaces that burn at 2,880 degrees. It's hard, unforgiving work that often goes unheralded. People rarely think about the human sacrifice that goes into steelmaking, that's involved when they step into their car, drive over a bridge, gawk up at skyscrapers, put some laundry in the dryer, or pop off the cap of a Starbucks drink at a convenience store. Much of the amenities and infrastructure we take for granted gets built in old industrial cities like Gary, factory towns where workers shower after work and not before. The metal you don't even notice but that's everywhere—in road signs, offices, hospitals, train stations— comes at a sometimes steep cost.

Gary Works, that steam-plume-shrouded steel mill that's all rust and rumbling semitrucks hauling off heavy steel coils to points unknown, remains a place where there's no guarantee you'll return home when you start your shift.

# HUBS AND HOMES

# Stay Debaucherous

## DAVID WEATHERSBY

from **Black in the Middle: An Anthology of the Black Midwest**

It was freezing, absolutely freezing. This was to be expected for mid-December in Chicago, but still, it was freezing. It was my third time around the same block as I searched for the deliberately covert address that I had just received four hours earlier. This was by design. It was a clever way of quite literally keeping the creeps away. This wasn't my first time at this event, but it was my first time since it had gained somewhat of a reputation. On my fourth pass, I was starting to wonder if there was going to be an event at all. I did notice a modest crowd starting to form around an unmarked door. I was desperate for any sign that I hadn't fallen victim to a massive GPS error, so I slowed down to see if the crowd would grow. I noticed more cars slowly pulling up to the location, each one pausing in front of this unmarked door, seemingly waiting for some sign of confirmation, just as I was.

I was confident enough at this point to park in the spot I had magically found and been idling in for twenty minutes. I was ready to brace the cold wind that was waiting for me outside of the car door. I had been a videographer in Chicago for some time at this point, so late nights and run-and-gun setups were a norm for me. With a combination of preparation and a bit of good fortune, I would get the footage I needed. This was years before I was producing documentaries, so I was not there for any ethnographical research adventure. I was simply asked to shoot the event by my friend Khari, and it was as much a fulfillment of curiosity as it was a video shoot. He had started the event as a way to celebrate his birthday, and I knew three things about it: it was secretive, they played house music, and it was called Thee Debauchery Ball.

As I gathered my equipment and started for the door, I noticed that knee-to-ankle-length coats were popular amongst the crowd waiting to get in. It was understandable due to the evening weather, but there was a sense of something clandestine in the air. We entered the elevator and rode up together with a low murmur of small talk until we arrived at our floor. As the doors opened, we rounded the corner into a typical office and studio building. We could feel the music before we heard it as the distant volume seemed to slowly rise in the room. The crowd around me began to shed their heavy coats, hats, and gloves, revealing an array of black, erotic clothing that ran the gamut from night-out sexy black dresses to body paint and very little (if anything) else.

We came to a table at the entrance of the last door in the hall. The woman at the table saw the camera in my hand along with all my accessories and waved me into the venue. I entered with only a spattering of light here and there to guide me. At first, I could only see the outlines of people— silhouettes against the shadowy background. As lights flickered and pulsated, I could see flashes of lace and skin. To my left, I caught a glimpse of glossy leather and metal accessories. Behind that, bright pink ropes were wrapped around a female figure who seemed almost oblivious to what was happening as she moved to the music. Before even turning on the camera, I scanned the room and saw a mass of Afro-eroticism and liberation. A ball-gagged woman wearing nothing but a sheer catsuit grooved in the same space as the masked woman covered in a cloak that did nothing to cover the pasties and black thong underneath. The room had a sense of unbridled sexuality with an overarching playful and consensual tone. This was clearly going to be . . . unconventional.

This was not the first party I had shot, and I never found them to be overly complicated. No matter how unique the host tried to make them, it came down to the same basic elements. Browse the room, look for the most expressive people, and search for those personal moments between individuals that tell a story of the event. But house music changes things. It moves differently. There's no preoccupation with a preset list of favorite songs but rather an indescribable moment of sounds based on the feel of the crowd and energy in the room. It speaks with each dancer in the room, and everyone responds whether they know it or not. That was my challenge: How do I find the personal moment in a room filled with personal moments?

I decided to start from one corner and work my way around the room, quietly navigating past the bodies in a personalized expression of inner sexuality. The loincloths around the masculine and feminine waists and black Gothic masks were accompanied by ankle-length cloaks and nude bodies, unless you count the body paint. My first stop was the corner of the venue that seemed to be designated for rope play. The bright pink rope that I had caught a glance of earlier was now spun around multiple women in various designs and configurations. It was easy to tell the difference between the curious and the experienced. Some looked on with a novice-like sense of wonder, and others settled into relaxed states that made it apparent this was definitely not their first time. I moved deeper into the venue and walked directly into fishnet stockings wrapped around the legs of a tall woman. As I scanned up and passed the black lingerie, I stopped at the cat-o'-nine-tails whip in her hand. Somehow, I didn't immediately see the willing participant bent over a chair, awaiting a moment of discipline. I was consumed with the figure and her commanding black whip. She playfully stalked her partner, staying with the beat of the music in the room. Light jabs became substantial hits that, with nonverbal consent, turned into heavy blows across the lower body. After one incredibly strong strike, the recipient stood and stared deeply at her whip-wielding aggressor. She took two steps forward and embraced her in an almost familial hug. Consent is beautiful.

I decided to follow the music and was struck by a tall, broad-shouldered figure toward the back of the venue. He stood behind a table filled with audio equipment, in full control of every sound coming out of the speakers. This was William Dunn, better known as DJ Big Will. To say Big Will makes an impression gives the word "understatement" new life. Living up to his moniker, he stands well past the six-foot mark, with shoulders that seem the same length and a booming voice that seemed audible even when the music drowned out any other sound. He was the head DJ and was there at the beginning when Khari was still forming the event. House music always revolves around the DJs, and each one speaks their own language with the tracks they select. Big Will's language was so pronounced and unique it was clearly the voice of Thee Debauchery Ball, and everyone seemed to understand it intimately.

Suddenly, all attention was directed to the front of the venue. A band had almost covertly set up while people were distracted by the music and were now trying to gather people around with a series of announcements, guitar riffs, and drum rhythms. People started to migrate toward the seating area around the band, some with a sense of anticipation and some with high levels of curiosity. The band built to a mix of funk, soul, and gospel music. Suddenly, a black-caped figure draped in silver Afrocentric jewelry took center stage. It was the man who had created everything I had experienced that night: Khari B.

I could describe Khari, I could find fancy words to explain to him as a person and an entertainer, but I tend to avoid futility. I will simply say that if a tempest of art, charisma, and unfiltered commentary formed into a sentient being, Khari would still be more interesting. Commonly carrying the title of the "Disco Poet," he has been a paragon of the city's art scene for as long as I can remember. Matter of fact, if you want to out yourself as a tourist, simply state, "I don't know who Khari B is."

But this night he was a musician as much as a poet. Backed by the all-female band of his own creation dubbed "Osun's Waters," he took the stage bare-chested but nearly concealed in glimmering silver Afrocentric necklaces, medallions, and bracelets. He warmed up the crowd with a combination of introductions, instructions, and jokes. The first song was a surprising mix of rock and poetry with an erotic tone, which seemed to be a summation of the event itself. Each transition from song to song seemed to evoke another genre of music, and each one had a unique poetic flow. I realized that this mix of genres was his nonverbal way of stating an overarching theme of the event and the culture around it. It's all house, it's all accepted, and it's all about community.

As the band began to wind down and peoples' attention turned back to the DJ, I was certain that I had captured enough footage for multiple projects, but I couldn't leave. I realized what I saw. I saw beauty, sexuality, no exploitation, no shame, judgments and inhibitions left at the door, and friends and lovers enjoying a safe space. There were stories upon stories, but one thing seemed clear—this was never just about sex, it was never just about lust. This was a living art exhibit, an exhibition of community freedom and expression. We need more of this whether we realize it or not.

As the final song played and lights were slowly turned on, I gathered my equipment and headed toward the exit with almost the same crowd I entered with at the beginning of this journey. We rounded the same corner and rode down in the same elevator. As I opened the door and was hit with the same Chicago winter air, I knew things were different. This needed to be documented, but its clandestineness needed to be protected. It needed to be celebrated and kept safe from those who would exploit it. But at that moment, in the frigid night air, one trivial thought would not leave my mind. I'm so glad I found parking.

# The Other "Forgotten People": Feeling Blue in Missouri

## SARAH KENDZIOR

from **Red State Blues: Stories from Midwestern Life on the Left**

In January 2016, shortly before the inauguration of Donald Trump, I was invited to a conference for people in the media and tech industries to discuss the future of news. Like every conference of this nature to which I've been invited, it was held in a city I could never afford to visit on my own, much less live—Palo Alto, California, where the average home sells for three million dollars. That would be two million, eight hundred and seventy thousand more than what the average home sells for where I live, in St. Louis, Missouri, a struggling, blue city in a once purple, suddenly bright-red state.

I arrived at the conference anxious to share my concerns about the future of media under Trump: the role Russian propaganda had played in the election, the mainstreaming of white supremacists by the national press, the gutting of local papers that had steered so many to conspiracy sites as an alternative.

These concerns, while shared by some attendees, were mostly dismissed, since the prevailing belief in blue, wealthy, tech-savvy California was that, somehow, democracy would work itself out. Once in office, Trump would surely be checked and balanced, they told me; freedom of the press could not seriously be challenged, as it was a constitutional right. What they were really struggling with, they said, was how to better understand "the red state people"—those poor, exploited midwesterners who had bought into Trump's fantasy and shocked the nation by propelling his win. Those poor, exploited midwesterners who had somehow—according to the coastal publishers and tech gurus in attendance—all suddenly become white, male, conservative manual laborers.

It is a terrible thing to be in pain and ignored—as a place, as an individual. It is perhaps worse to finally be recognized, but only as a symbol—to be given a mask and told that it's your face.

This is what it has been like to be both a member of the national media and a citizen of the Midwest since Trump's win, as the coastal media views our long-ignored region through a narrow journalistic kaleidoscope, twisting and turning on the same images again and again until the view is utterly distorted. It is true that the national media—so disproportionately represented by the coasts that one out of every five journalists now lives in New York, Los Angeles, or Washington, DC—had long ignored the white, male, conservative manual laborers of the Midwest. But now, apparently, their plan was to ignore everyone else who lived there too: Black, Brown, Muslim and Jewish citizens; workers who toiled not in a field or plant but in a Walmart or a university; intellectuals and immigrants; and anyone else who was appalled at the election of Donald Trump. We lived in Trumpland now, we were told, and our blue city was an inconvenient island.

In some sense, this dynamic is not new. For decades, as national media consolidated on the coasts and regional papers died out, the Midwest got used to being ignored. The national media would show interest when there was a disaster—a tornado, a murder, an act of negligence so spectacular it would merit the occasional check-in (Flint still doesn't have water, by the way), or, in the case of 2016, a grotesque election. Now, due to surprising Republican wins in Michigan, Wisconsin, and Pennsylvania, alongside more predictable wins in every state but Illinois and Minnesota, the Midwest was suddenly standing in as Trump's mandate. This, of course, was a lie: the Midwest boasts an incredibly diverse array of citizens held together, perversely, by little other than a shared sense of neglect. We are not red or blue but mixed, purple like a bruise. But that wasn't the kind of pain or complexity the national press typically examines—not an individual level, where the ambiguity of lackluster choices propelled votes certainly as much as fanaticism; and not on a structural level, where the irregularities of our voting system have left the legitimacy of the election somewhat in doubt.

With a few exceptions, the national press was not interested in the gerrymandering that had plagued our states for decades, or the new voter ID laws that disenfranchised over two hundred thousand people in states like Wisconsin, where Trump won by a miniscule margin of roughly twenty thousand votes. They were not particularly interested in how Trump won—that is, in structural barriers that challenge the narrative of ideological conformity within the Midwest—but in who Trump claimed as the "new winners" of his America, the "forgotten people" whom he claimed to have uniquely remembered. In order for the self-conscious coastal press to lay claim to Trump's narrative—to prove that they were not, as he claimed, the "media elite"—another group needed to be forgotten for Trump's "forgotten people" to shine.

And that group of "forgotten people" was the group that remains an inconvenience to everyone: the mostly liberal, often nonwhite residents of the Midwest's sprawling cities, where people are far more likely to work in the service industry than in the manufacturing fields Trump presented as the heart of the "real America." That heart was torn out decades ago, and while Trump was correct in identifying the pain of that economic loss and the social upheaval in its wake, he showed no understanding or even interest in our current plight.

And why would he? Blue city midwesterners were, by and large, not his people. Blue city midwesterners were, to his horror, his protesters—the people most likely to see through Trump's bullshit due to a lifetime spent navigating an abundance of bullshit in their midst; the people most likely to see Trump's autocratic policies not as horrifying fantasies but as a federally instituted implementation of what they had witnessed on a local level for a very long time.

When Trump arrived in St. Louis for his first rally in March 2016, he was greeted by a large, ethnically diverse array of protesters, including members of long-standing citizen movements fighting for higher wages, LGBT rights, and, especially after Ferguson, an end to racist police brutality. Having suffered under local and state repressive policies, this was not a group of people who would take Donald Trump in stride or dismiss him as a joke or a long shot. St. Louis was the first city to shut a Trump rally down, though Chicago got the credit after his appearance there was canceled hours later.

As the campaign wore on and Trump's team began proposing a series of measures so autocratic that many pundits dismissed them as unfathomable, urban Missourians countered that this was indeed possible: Trump was merely a variant on what we had known. (You may recall we spent the bulk of November 2014 under martial law.) And life has only gotten worse for us since. The 2016 election turned the Missouri legislature overwhelmingly Republican, and they have passed policies so sadistic that outsiders often mistake them for a sick joke: lowering the hourly minimum wage from $10.00 to $7.70; being so racist the NAACP gave Missouri a travel warning and told Black people not to visit; passing a law making it possible for your boss to fire you if he discovers you are taking birth control; being one of very few states to give private citizens' voting data to the Trump administration under the pretense of countering "fraud," and so on.

Often thought of as an irrelevant backwater, Missouri is arguably a harbinger of America's brutal future under Trump. We are indeed the "Show-Me State," as in, Trump says "Show Me" and our legislature of lackeys—in violation of basic democratic norms and laws—complies.

As I write this, the Trump administration is considering an array of policies that mirror those Missouri has managed to pass on a local level. These policies will disproportionately affect the red state voters about which he pretends to care. His tax plan will raise taxes most on households making $75,000 or under, meaning the bulk of states affected are in the Midwest or the South instead of the wealthier blue states on the coast. The possible repeal of Obamacare similarly hurts red state voters, who are poorer and more poorly served by their state governments in terms of receiving basic medical care than blue states. If net neutrality is eliminated, the vast rural stretches of the Midwest that are already denied affordable broadband access will find their prices raised even more, while midwestern media—already gutted—may die out completely if fewer residents can afford to access it.

We are in an incredible amount of trouble out here in the red state of Missouri, and over the past year, there have been an incredible number of protests in our blue cities—and even in our redder cities in the Ozarks, like Springfield—that reflect this anxiety. Missourians have protested against low wages, for women's rights, for immigrants' rights, for LGBT rights, for Black rights, for a full investigation of the Russian interference scandal, for science, for health care, for tax transparency, and more. Indivisible and other new activist groups have joined an already robust protest and organizational infrastructure. This is a painful fight, as we watch our friends and neighbors lose their civil and economic rights, but it is one to which we are sadly accustomed.

But it is a fight that is scarcely covered by the national press. It was only after the neo-Nazi Charlottesville that the media began to consider that it wasn't "economic anxiety" that guided the Trump case after all. This is not to say that people in red states don't have economic anxiety—pretty much everyone does, given that the recession never really ended here.

But that does not seem to be what attracts Trump's hard-core base—and furthermore, that hard-core base is not particularly representative of the electorate even in red states like Missouri. Trump's numbers sit as a record low, while protests against a sitting president occur, arguably, at a record high. That story remains largely untold in my state, along with the fear and determination that propels those attempting to hold the administration accountable.

In January 2016, in Palo Alto, an executive at a major media company asked me how to capture what's really going on in the red states. My answer was simple: "Hire locals," I said. "Don't send parachute journalists. Hire people who live there year-round, who know the system, who have a stake in what happens, who strangers will trust because they won't really be strangers."

He laughed. "But we can't do that," he said. "I mean, we need to hire intelligent people. We need people who know how to write."

I told him I lived in St Louis and smiled, and he blanched, perhaps because I had proven Missouri journalists are real, perhaps because he was startled I still had all my teeth. He then asked if I'd be interested in writing about "rural life" and I explained I lived in a metropolitan area of nearly three million people and he should find someone who actually lives in a rural area. He stared at me blankly, and I felt that familiar sense of rage—the rage, horribly, that Trump had tapped into, the rage of being condescended to and ignored.

That rage is still burning in Missouri, where, as usual, we in the blue cities have learned that we have to fight our own battles—because many of the people in the coastal blue states think we do not deserve support, and because our own state government holds us in contempt. We are fighting as much for conservative residents as we are for fellow progressives, as many structural injustices—economic inequality, health care, the right to free speech and media—affect everyone. We are fighting against what's coming, because for us—the blue voters in the red states, the other forgotten people of Trump's America—the grim future has already arrived.

# South Shore: Between the Lake and Emmett Till Road

AUDREY PETTY

from **The Chicago Neighborhood Guidebook**

From the outset, we knew a big house wouldn't do. Togetherness was the whole idea, but we'd need separate kitchens, bathrooms, and front doors with their own locks for the arrangement to last. We were on the lookout for at least three stories.

Hyde Park–Kenwood was our starting point in the search for a family building. After all, my brother-in-law worked in the neighborhood; my sister Jill and I had grown up there, and my husband Maurice had, too. For decades, my father had made his home in Kenwood with my mother, who'd died a few months before we embarked upon our search. Her illness had brought me back to Chicago from central Illinois. The comfort of the familiar was profound. What had sometimes been tiresome about being back in the old neighborhood was suddenly balm. Within close reach were those who would claim me, those who could remember when. To my initial disappointment, the Hyde Park survey went bust quickly. Three-flats were few and far between, and prices were steep, so our search spread to North Kenwood, Woodlawn, Bronzeville. The search lasted two seasons.

Early on, we visited a new construction on Kimbark, due south of the University of Chicago. How I hated that one at first glance. Narrow, newfangled, formed of split-face concrete block. What passed for its decorative front was faux stone veneer, straight-up ugly and soulless, resistant to any change. From the inside, the building made okay sense. The floor plans met our needs. The kids could grow up there. I could see it all when I closed my eyes.

We'd move on to consider a pricey and decrepit redbrick six-flat on Ellis—the light there barely light at all, but its backyard was double-wide, immense, promising. We toured an imposing graystone in Bronzeville divvied into odd-shaped units, near-kitchenettes. We lingered long inside a three-flat on Langley, bordered by an empty lot and stripped down to the studs. So many prospects we encountered seemed viable to me, but fortunately, we were a five-headed, deliberative body, weighing each listing quite carefully. My father, who drove the hardest bargain, encouraged us to consider ditching him at every turn. "You all should do what you need to do. I'll figure my own thing out." We wouldn't move without him.

We finally arrived at our family building on the day my dad took his time on the walk-through—when he strolled each floor instead of making a clean exit, detouring to wait for us in the car. To be sure, the summer drive from Hyde Park to South Shore—to Oglesby Avenue—had set the stage for our unanimity: Lake Shore Drive, past the museum, the beach house at Sixty-Third, around the bend at Jackson Park Harbor, the public golf course running along our passenger side. We paused to admire our future building from outside. Elegant, made of true brick and stone with craft and with care. Quoins flanked the sides of its stories, and crowning the building was the emblem of a ribbon—festoon—near center, and a concrete urn on the far left.

The interior of this one had been nearly entirely reworked. As Redfin revealed, the sellers had purchased the residence, erected in 1922, on the very cheap, in a tax sale. Now these sellers were flipping it, aiming to bank a nearly eightfold profit; this was a pattern amongst the many buildings we'd seen, a phenomenon of what realtors dubbed *the post-crisis bottom*. To my eye, so much of precious value at Oglesby had been excised by *rehab*; that the sellers were white *and* faraway added insult to injury. They'd stripped place out of the place, scrapping sconces, tilework, and, likely—from the looks of our neighbors' buildings—leaded windows and chandeliers. In return, they'd been heavy-handed with recessed lighting and cheap, domed fixtures. They'd installed faux fireplaces run by remote control.

Still, somehow (how?), by day's end, the building was what we all wanted. I suppose we thought as much of what could be as what had been, in making up our minds. And I sought out vestiges upon our second-look visit. Polished hardwood, a set of French doors, crown molding in the dining rooms. "From my floor, I've got a treehouse," my father told us from the first-floor unit. He stood in place for a while, peering out at lovely, lively Hasan Park.

We moved into our place in the late fall of 2012. We met neighbors in the family buildings on either side of us, three generations deep, in South Shore for decades. And Hasan Park was soon our front yard living room, no matter the miserable temperatures. Ella, five, and Malcolm, six, climbed, slid, and raced with their rambunctious set while we paced and shivered with fellow caregivers. We'd become acquainted with more folks at community organizing meetings, brought together by multiple crises. O'Keefe was our nearest elementary school, and its entire staff had been fired and replaced. Fermi Elementary, about a mile to the west, was one of fifty neighborhood schools slated for permanent closure. Our local Dominick's would also be shuttering, leaving the closest full-service grocery two miles away.

Soon, I'd meet Sylvia. A mom and grandmother and former eighteen-wheeler trucker, she made a living as a registered CNA and a part-time caterer. This work was balanced with organizing and creating events for nourishment and fellowship in her neighborhood of Park Side, an area of South Shore where many people displaced by the demolition of high-rise public housing relocated. Sylvia organized Peace Fests, gospel concerts, and movie screenings in abandoned lots; she cooked an annual Christmas buffet that was accompanied by a gift giveaway. She also prepared enormous feasts in the warm months, making the occasion for what she calls Community Feeds. Sylvia's grandparents had migrated to Chicago as young adults. Her mother's people came from Louisiana. Her father's people came from Tennessee and Mississippi. As a girl, Sylvia lived in Wentworth Gardens, then and now public housing. And this is where she first learned about community gardens. Southern folks came up with this know-how, she told me, and at Wentworth Gardens, their gardens once thrived.

Sometimes we'd head out after dinner, just the three of us, scaling the wall bordering the sidewalk at Sixty-Seventh and the public golf course. Atop that wall, we'd inch toward wild mulberry, with Maurice holding Ella steady and high. As she grabbed and tasted the sweetness, I made peace with rose-purpley stains, the only price for what my husband called "goodney." From there, we'd pass across the tended lawn, saluting the golfers we'd startle, and then it was on to the tangle of bramble, on to the edge of Lake Michigan. Ella was strong and confident enough to take her own stony path safely down to the water. Back then, we called the place Turkey Burger Beach. The slabs of red-brown slag were our roomy perches before the lake. Quiet beach. Unofficial beach. Free of flags and unattended by lifeguards. The north skyline Oz-like. To the south: the smokestacks of Gary Steelworks. Straight ahead: lake and sky melded. That first summer the beach was magnetic. *Can you believe it?* Nearby and magnificent, still grieving the death of my mother, the lake was my tonic. Choppy or still. Arm's length away. Numbingly cold and piercing and wondrous.

We'd measure our time in South Shore by the hidden beach's changes. The second summer would be the summer of thick dragonflies hovering. There'd be the summer of the coyote dashing away from the brush. And, of course, the near constant occasions: those many weeks of high *E. coli* count and keeping bacteria test strips in my shoulder bag. We'd meet regulars. A trio of middle-aged Polish women from the Southwest Side, always sunning and swimming for entire Saturdays with a transistor radio, folding chairs, and small overflowing picnic basket in tow. At dusk on weekdays: a young man in a white thobe and turban, praying on a limestone ledge.

When a visiting friend from Atlanta made the stroll to the beach with us, he'd ask how we could afford all of this beauty. My husband and I would try to explain Chicago-style white flight and the Black Belt, and how Chicago segregation persists—how we'd come to know and feel the city's ironclad segregation. If a Chicago neighborhood was Black enough, it would stay Black, we'd attest. This seemed as certain to us as the lake being east. What we didn't acknowledge was Black Chicago was rapidly shrinking. Maurice and I were children of the second wave of the Great Migration. Ella and Malcolm arrived in the time of the Great Exodus.

In 2018, as summer was ending, we scaled the wall at Sixty-Seventh and South Shore Drive with Ella and her friend and classmate, who's also our neighbor. It had been over a month since Chicago police had shot and killed Harith Augustus, a neighborhood barber, on busy East Seventy-First Street. The mulberry tree had already yielded its fruit. The golf course was vacant, pristine. On the beach, Ella and Cosima were boisterous, skipping rocks and tapping the lake with their fingertips. In the weeks since we'd last been there, the shoreline was changed. Many slabs were disappeared, swallowed. The few that remained had been shoved aside by currents; the biggest of them all hosted green shoots. Maurice marveled out loud at the power of the lake, while we studied a strange iron bracket at the shore's edge. Whatever it meant to contain, it was going to rust, loosening, on the cusp of drifting out. The beach wasn't our final destination that day. I'd been meaning to finally visit the Nature Conservancy behind the South Shore Country Club. I was well overdue.

The next day, early morning, Ella and I headed to our favorite bakery, seeking a large cake, a pie. What we found instead was a case full of miniatures: sweet potato pies and peach cobblers, pecan bar slices, key lime squares. We asked for two of everything, and while we waited, we breathed the sweet air deeply. I tried to convince Ella that smelling cooking butter and sugar was halfway to tasting dessert for free. She disagreed, and, to my surprise, declined my offer of any choice of treat. "Gift?" the clerk asked as she set our box on the counter. Nervously, realizing my nervousness, I paid.

Pulling up to Sidelines Studio, I noticed the red and white sign in the window.

"HIRING LICENSED BARBER," it announced. Ella carried the box and I held the door. We said hello to everyone in the shop as we entered. One barber was sweeping. The other finished trimming the beard of a young man whose gaze was fixed on the TV overhead.

"We're your neighbors," I told the sweeping barber, whose face I recognized from the news. He'd organized the vigil. "We wanted you to know we've been thinking about you." I tried to find the words as I introduced myself. "We want to share our condolences. For Snoop. For Harith. We've been thinking about him. We've been thinking about you all." He hugged me tightly and then he bent down to Ella. "What's your name, little sis?" he asked as they reached out to each other.

# Flea Market Urbanism

### SAMANTHA SANDERS

from **Midwest Architecture Journeys**

If you set out to write a certain kind of story about Monroe, Ohio (population 12,442), you might begin by drawing attention to its city newspaper (online only), *Main Street Monroe*, and its front page that prominently features a church directory and a post about a Dairy Queen coming to town. Maybe you'd mention the article about the initiative from the local Carpenters Union meant to address the "skilled labor shortages [that] continue to plague Ohio contractors" and contextualize it within a larger story—maybe the one about the dearth of trade education, or the one about the unforeseen effects of immigration crackdown.

This would be, after all, a story told during what we'll have no choice but to refer to in coming years as the Trump Years, when newspaper editors from both coasts deservedly caught flak for airdropping reporters into places like Ohio purely for the sound-bite potential, before promptly scooping them back up again.

You might note that Monroe, which straddles both sides of Interstate 75 and is nearly equidistant to both Cincinnati and Dayton, sits at the far edge of Butler County, home to author J. D. Vance and the setting for his bestselling *Hillbilly Elegy*, a fact that will likely elicit either a solemn nod or an exaggerated eye roll, depending on the reader's politics.

But I'm from the area, too. And stories preoccupied with the past have never sat right with me, largely because that past was rarely as romantic as whatever present is being unfairly compared to it. The Midwest is as dynamic a place as any other, and for as much is made of it being a dying place, its outsiders would be better served by thinking of the place as a massive iterative process; repeating cycles and processes, living with their outcomes, before beginning again, each time maybe moving closer to a kind of perfection. And if that's not hope, I don't know what is.

And for all the dismissive terms that speak to the supposed sameness of the culture, or to the empty blandness of the natural and manmade geography of the place (flyover country, land of big box stores, the cloyingly sweet "heartland"), there remains an impulse, as in all places, but especially in those where vast land filled with endless acres of geometrically rigid and inhumanly scaled cash crops threatens to swallow you up. That impulse is to gather together. Main Street is on the ropes, but midwesterners have long had another outlet to meet this basic human need for connection: the flea market.

And while it's true that fleas flank the highways along exurban edges all across the country, there's something uniquely midwestern about the character of the flea—the industriousness of bringing product to market, the weekend excursion ritual of it, the chance to see and be seen in places where that's a relative rarity, the angling for a deal, the validation that your nostalgia for knickknacks means *something*, even if that something remains an undefined feeling.

Any thrifter or flea enthusiast knows the feeling that accompanies a trip. The anxious sensation in the stomach or the impulse to stop by the bathrooms near the entrance so you won't get distracted later. You are, after all, on a mission, and today could be the day you find something great. In the Midwest, the flea is a vernacular expression of longing and hope, nurtured by a common history, spurred by a collective boredom, and all sheltered by a pole barn down by the highway.

Save your entry ticket. There'll be a raffle later.

---

Long before the outlet malls came to Monroe, before the truck stops went corporate and got cleaner, and before AK Steel took its jobs and left, there was Traders World Market, a massive indoor flea market my parents would take me to most weekends when I was a kid. To give you an idea of the scale, its website describes it (currently) as "16 buildings, 850 inside vendor spaces, 400 outdoor vendor spaces, a combined area of 11 acres, plenty of paved parking and over two miles of store fronts." In my memories, it is even bigger.

As a kid, I'd feel the excitement build on the drive there. It took about twenty minutes, which to my kid brain felt just long enough to qualify as a true outing; a step above a trip to the mall, a few rungs below an amusement park. For a while in the early 2000s, if you'd taken the same route, you'd have passed the megachurch that erected a sixty-two-foot statue of Jesus along the eastern edge of I-75. Officially titled "King of Kings," it was more colloquially known as "Touchdown Jesus" for its outstretched arms raised heavenward, until a lightning strike and resulting fire arrived in 2010.

Still, there's plenty to look at. The land surrounding Traders World is orderly; rows of soybean and corn, the area's two largest crops. The methodicalness of it is obvious, even at ground level doing seventy. The environment here is something to be disciplined because so much depends on it.

Visitors approaching the massive complex must drive first through the front gate, underneath two massive statues of horses rearing up on their hind legs. A couple bucks paid to the parking lot attendant earns you access to a massive sea of concrete, where you can leave your car behind, making careful note of the number of the building you slip into.

Walking into one of those buildings is like walking into a photo relief of the world outside. Inside is dark, cavernous, and the air-conditioning feels crisp and merciful in the summertime. And there are people, a critical mass of them, everywhere. And they're walking. I grew up riding my bike to the entrance of our subdivision and back, tethered by my mom's warnings to not go farther. It was a thrilling but limited kind of freedom. I was separated from any places I might want to walk or bike to on my own by miles of sidewalk-less streets where cars were the only thing you'd expect to see on the road. It made sense, since you weren't getting anywhere without one.

And the majority of America is car dependent, so to be a kid, navigating the weekend crowds of people at the flea was an unfamiliar but exciting feeling. Inside, the rows of stalls promised potentiality around every corner. And even though most people put out the same things at their booth every week—bins of tube socks, boxes of farm tomatoes, moldering issues of *Life Magazine*—I still felt a thrill at what I might find.

Outside, the vendors were day renters, usually selling produce or seemingly random assortments of everyday items you might find at garage sales: old magazines, collectible plates, that one olive green Pyrex casserole dish with the white daisy pattern that seemed like it followed me everywhere as a kid. Inside, the vendors were there for the long haul. The majority of the booths—the leather Harley gear, the sneaker place, the food stalls—stayed in place all week, only to open for a few hours each weekend. The whole place was built as a series of long wings coming off a central hub, where dozens of picnic-style tables were set up around the few roller-skating-rink-grade food options. In the center of it all, a man in lederhosen played accordion to polka backing tracks with pre-recorded backup vocals so lifelike that when he sang, "I don't want her / You can have her / She's too fat for me / HEY! She's too fat for me," it sounded like a dozen men proclaiming it while you sat and ate your roller grill hot dog.

Shopping at a flea was a markedly different feeling than shopping at, say, a mall, that other defining feature of the countryside and the era. A mall felt purposeful; you were there to buy things. A visit to the flea felt more free-form. You were there as much to move through the space and experience the surroundings as you were to pick through the merchandise. And in an era before big box bookstores or teenagers hanging out at Starbucks, *the flea was a true third place*. You didn't have to buy. You could just *be*.

———

It might initially seem odd to consider the flea market from an architectural perspective. After all, most fleas are the kind of depressing, pre-fab and post-frame construction you usually see in down-market self-storage facilities. But if vernacular architecture can be said to respond to the needs of its environment and be made with what's at hand, I can't think of a kind of building that speaks more to the part of the Midwest where I grew up than the sturdy-if-unsightly pole buildings that house many of the fleas I know. These pre-fab buildings are relatively easy to build, economical, and the architectural equivalent of meat and potatoes, all utility and short on garnish. While at a distance, they may be nearly indistinguishable from the big box stores and mall husks that flank the highways, they function in a very different way.

In these places, it's important to consider that architecture is as much about the physical manifestation of our ideals as it is about the materials used. We didn't have a Main Street where I grew up. Fewer and fewer small towns do now, as big boxes supplant and core out a wider and wider range of small business storefronts, so we made a new Main Street, albeit in the form of a flea, with paid parking and air-conditioning. And like a Main Street, the fleas function as a space to experience some sort of civic awareness and community as a place to buy something.

It's no surprise that in an era of online shopping and the heavily curated feeds of Instagram influencers, the shopping mall, with its cookie-cutter stores and limited selection, is quickly becoming a relic. It's true that flea markets often have footprints as large, if not larger than those of the typical mall, and fleas are rarely planted in the same kind of sought-after land most commercial real estate is after. Further, fleas' limited hours and distance from cities often require a dedicated consumer—presenting what a retail wonk might call a "barrier to purchase."

Yet given all that, the mood on the National Flea Market Association website is bullish if not downright combative; 2.25 million vendors, it trumpets, over $30 billion in sales annually, more than 150 million customers each year. And the number of fleas? More than 1,100.

We've reached a point in American retail history where—if not now, then soon—flea markets will outnumber malls. Given everything we know, this shouldn't make sense within the context of where retail is headed. But it does within the context of where America is headed.

Traders World was founded by a couple named Jay and Helen Frick about thirty years ago (the website is a bit confusing on the official date, and requests for interviews were not answered). And while that only takes us back to the late 1980s, you'd never guess that from the way the Fricks (or whoever authored the website's History page) talk about it. The Fricks "grew up in the unique era of Americana [sic]," the introductory paragraph explains, handily if accidentally leapfrogging the concept of America-as-a-country in favor of landing right in my sweet spot: Americana-as-culture.

The Traders World site goes on to explain that this was a time "when lives were transitioning from agricultural farm living to industrialized urban living. It was a time that spanned from the depths of the Great Depression to the booming years that followed World War II—a time in American history that some refer to as 'the greatest generation.'" I'm calling this out not to dunk on the sentimentality of a couple who built a place that brought me so much joy but to note that by mythologizing their past through the flea's marketing and decor, the Fricks are following the blueprint of so many fleas that have found success by commoditizing our collective nostalgia.

Traders World was thick with bric-a-brac. Long before I ever set foot in a Cracker Barrel, I knew what it was like to sit in a dark, wood-paneled room eating fried food underneath a rusty scythe, or a repro tin sign advertising spark plugs. Often, the only way I could remember how to find my way back to the entrance where I came in was to find the particular folksy woodcut hanging from the ceiling I could last recall ("AT QUIZ PA AINT NO WHIZ BUT HE KNOWS HOW TO KEEP MA HIZ").

The website also explains that Helen's earliest memories "included plowing the fields with horses, planting the crops by hand—sometimes one seed at a time; and sleigh bells on a team of horses gliding effortlessly through the snow on a winter's night." I suspect I'm not alone in being drawn to fleas because they evoke a world I never knew but have been told was more authentic, more tangible, better than my own.

But to take that view might not be giving the flea its full credit. The past is compelling, but the present is, too. In fact, flea markets are an awfully good indicator of how our culture and economy are changing—and being changed.

---

As Rob Sieban, CEO of United Flea Markets, explained recently, "The value proposition [of flea markets] is evolving." For him, that means opportunity. Where we might see nostalgia, a private equity firm might look at flea markets, often family-run operations, and see motivated sellers (perhaps a second or third generation not as eager to run a flea as their parents may have been), comparatively affordable real estate, and reliable income from vendor space that might be an easier rental than a traditional mall's lease.

Which is to say: Today's third places are becoming increasingly commodified. From POPS, or Publicly Owned Private Spaces (think of the blandly inviting plazas outside corporate buildings), where your presence is tolerated as a zoning-mandated means to an end, to Edison-bulbed coworking spaces whose spare Scandinavian aesthetic can now be seen from Stockholm to St. Louis and everywhere in between, we've begun to passively accept that our presence must generate revenue for someone. And while flea markets may never (fortunately) be top-of-mind to most private equity groups hoping to make a buck, there is something to be said for the ways in which flea market entrepreneurship offers a real leg up for some vendors who will never be invited to sell their wares at a pop-up celebrating a new boutique hotel opening.

And there's plenty of evidence fleas are becoming important parts of local economies, serving as de facto business incubators in places as yet untouched by the entrepreneurship-as-spirituality crowd. Not every product makes sense to sell in an online Etsy store, but there's a decent chance at a flea that you might get a passerby to impulse-buy some laser-cut floor mats for their Silverado.

Fleas are often an ideal place for would-be restaurateurs who aren't yet food truck-ready to test their concept. When there are some pretty significant steps between you and a brick and mortar location, fleas are a low-stakes place to dream unwieldy, impractical dreams. Or even very practical ones that mainstream culture may be blind to. The last few times I've been to Traders World, I was heartened to see that it had grown into not just a place where the local Hispanic population was beginning to visit, they were also selling. Fleas that recreate the *mercados de pulgas* of Latin America have long been a fixture of life in parts of the country with large Hispanic populations, but as the Midwest's Hispanic population grows, stores inside these fleas (particularly in very rural areas or those where immigration is relatively recent) can serve as both lifelines to culture and as a parallel economy in places where goods from home might be hard to come by.

---

Whether a given item for sale at a flea is a treasure is highly subjective, and maybe my can't-miss booth is one your eyes might quickly scan past. But I'll always appreciate the egalitarianism of landing a vendor's spot at the fleas I remember as a kid. It's true that urban fleas, while long a fixture in some cities, have started to pop up all over. But their curated sameness depresses me. I hesitate to write about how there's always a beard-oil guy because in a few years, I wonder if I'll even remember what this was. But he's there, along with the handmade-soap lady and someone selling bird art suitable for framing. I wonder what we're saying with our current hyper-specific cultural bric-a-brac. Which of it will be picked over, suddenly hip again, at future fleas? Which of it will be some ten-year-old's inescapable olive green Pyrex twenty years from now?

I don't live in Ohio anymore. I'm no longer a regular at Traders World. But fleas will always serve as a tether to home for me, no matter where I am. And for many people—especially those with perhaps more drive than creditworthiness and more ideas than square feet, fleas are much more than just symbolic, they're a livelihood. For people who might feel alone during the week, they're culture. And for people who just want to spend time in a place that's not work or home, they're a quirky kind of public sphere. And as the culture changes, the population shifts, and the economy fluctuates, fleas will adapt. In that way, they'll be a bellwether of the Midwest. One foot in the past, one in the future, but always with ample parking, just off I-75, past Touchdown Jesus.

# Photos by
# LaToya Ruby Frazier

from **The Pittsburgh Anthology**

Along the ancient path of the Monongahela River, Braddock, Pennsylvania, sits in the eastern region of Allegheny County, approximately nine miles outside of Pittsburgh. A historic industrial suburb, Braddock is home to Andrew Carnegie's first steel mill, the Edgar Thomson Works, which has operated since 1875 and is the last functioning steel mill in the region.

The apparition is me.
We are not in Manet's bar at the Folies-Bergère.

On Fridays, I'd walk with Grandma Ruby to the fish market to buy black bass, and if she had money left over, we'd get lady locks and thumbprint cookies from Guenther's Bakery. Sometimes on Saturdays we'd wait for the 56B in front of Braddock News to take the PAT bus over to Eighth Avenue in Homestead and transfer to the 55M for a two-hour bus ride out to Century III Mall in West Mifflin.

The collapse of the steel industry throughout the 1970s and 1980s limited upward mobility. A majority of us would never own our homes and businesses or gain access to higher education or better jobs. For generations, we inherited debts we did not owe.

Our husbands, brothers, sons, and boyfriends were relegated to menial wage jobs, underemployment, or layoffs. Undermined by the mainstream economy, social isolation kept them company.

Across a hard metal counter, she laid there. Her head was propped up. Her lips were glued shut. Her skin looked thin and smooth. She looked like a porcelain doll.

While the Pittsburgh Steelers celebrated victory and Obama danced with Michelle, I clutched on to the handle with two hands. The rubber from my sneakers kept slipping on the wet snow. I clenched my teeth. In my mind I could hear her say, "You better not drop me, Toy."

I stepped up over the plot. The funeral director instructed me to slowly kneel and release the handles. My side was off. I pushed the coffin until it was straight.

# It Is Not Waste All This, Not Placed Here in Disgust, Street after Street

KATHLEEN ROONEY

from **Rust Belt Chicago**

*The city is dangerous and cannot be trusted.*

We are making our way through the city to find a knife, but I don't know that yet. So far we are drifting, the destination a surprise.

"We" are my flâneur friend Eric and I; "the city" is Chicago, gray with an azure tinge and snowy.

The knife is not because the city is dangerous, though. It will turn out to be tiny, the size of a single Cheeto, a classic Swiss Army knife, half-red, with its Victorinox crossbearing cover long ago cracked off, aluminum alloy and brass rivets exposed. A one of a kind—like the city here, now. And the knife will actually come to prove the opposite: that the city can be safe and the city can be trustworthy.

*The city is dangerous and cannot be trusted* is something that we—Eric and I and everyone, really—are told all the time.

In *The Death and Life of Great American Cities*, Jane Jacobs says that, "cities are, by definition, full of strangers." How one feels about strangers and their strangeness probably determines how one feels about cities. Me, I love them—strangers and cities. So did Jane Jacobs. Eric loves cities too, and strangers—but only as strangers.

We are taking the Red Line from the far North Side—Rogers Park for him, Edgewater for me—and I know we are heading to the Loop, but I don't know why. He has told me only that we are looking for something of his that he left in public a long time ago and he doesn't know if it will still be there. He is "confident but not hopeful." He refuses to tell me what the object is, or where, because that would spoil our trip for me, turning it from flânerie into just another holiday errand to accomplish in haste.

My father is a hunter and so am I—spending hours on icy days traversing the snowy scapes in search of.

My father's terrain is rural Nebraska—mine, urban Chicago. My father carries a gun—I, an iPhone camera.

Though my walks are year-round, I think of my father's hunting only in winter because winter is the season for his target animals: pheasants and quail. Feral cats, too, which he shoots when he sees them, hating the way they decimate the songbirds, the way the cats kill not just to eat but also for sport (hypocrisy, yes, but don't try to tell my dad that).

What I'm hunting for today—the day of the knife—and every day I walk is a certain sensation of being in the city, being like total presence, and a certain sensation of being out of time. Not like running out of time as with a finite resource but existing outside of time, floating above it or flowing with it, being aware of and seeing it but from the perspective of a bird riding a thermal above a river. Affected by time but not how most humans are; not how I am for most of the rest of my nonwalking life.

We emerge from the subway at Lake Street, in front of the Macy's that for 154 years was Marshall Field's, where a Salvation Army bell ringer is ringing and ringing because it's almost Christmas.

*The city is dangerous and cannot be trusted* is something you are told all the time because somebody benefits by having you think that.

Because of their capacity to encourage frequent serendipitous interaction between large numbers of extremely diverse people, cities have always been engines of radical social change. Fear slows the engine. People and institutions who oppose radical social change benefit by manufacturing fear of the city: corporations that want cheap labor and profit from people's distress, municipal institutions that justify their existences by their claim to control and protect.

Fear Los Gallos, trust Chipotle. Embrace the Bed, the Bath, but never the too far Beyond. Division Street, yes, but only east of Roberto Clemente.

A flâneur knows that the wrong way to use the city is actually the right way. That to journey to the elevated-train-circumscribed financial heart of Chicago during business hours on a Monday neither to work, nor to shop, nor to sightsee is to move against its efficiencies and capitalistic tendencies. That to use the city incorrectly is to correct some of the city's undeniable imbalances.

Flâneurs never run—late or otherwise.

Flâneurs never get lost because they're not going anywhere.

Flâneurs like Eric lead you from the sidewalk up the wooden stairs to the overhead platform, still at Lake but now above the street itself, where the Pink, Purple, Green, Brown, and Orange lines all converge. The Orange Line has just arrived. The platform is flooded with shoppers, commuters, holiday tourists.

Flâneurs thread you through the crowd to the edge of the platform, where a large, locked, metal newspaper-recycling box sits. They crouch, remove their mitten, and reach around and behind and under the container. They scratch into rotted wood crusted with grime and ice. Is it here? Has it survived? Then they smile and hold up the object, the unknown thing you've come to find: the palm-sized red Swiss Army knife, all its attachments still intact, unharmed, and unrusted, just as they left it.

City as time capsule, to be opened before or after our demise, in a month, in a decade, in an hour. Now, here, or never. This patch of sidewalk has been waiting for our eyes since 1948. That stone might be older than ancient Egypt.

Even the skies above the city are dangerous and cannot be trusted, which is why Eric had to think fast. He was on his way, November 23, the week of Thanksgiving, to Midway Airport and aware that they might not let him take the knife aboard his flight, so when he transferred from the Red to the Orange Line, he stowed it.

In the Loop, out of the Loop, the city is ours. We help build it with our eyes, our ears, our minds, and our hearts. Across the river from Ozinga Concrete. Under the Dan Ryan. On the Metra tracks. Cermak west of Western. Ogden south of Cicero. Milwaukee north of Belmont. Thirty-Fifth east of Wabash. The sublime wasteland stretching south to Chinatown from Roosevelt Road.

The city is multifunctional and opens like the knife. The knife is a weapon, or the knife is a tool. Fear lets you see only the weapon. Unfear lets you see and trust the tool.

The truth is: you can hide something in the city, in the broad light of the public eye, abandon it for weeks of dark nights all alone in the winter, and then return to it.

The city hides itself, waiting for you to return to it.

And the city is not your enemy. The city is nobody's enemy. It is something that rewards respect and grace and careful attention. At our respective ages and demographics, Eric and I are ninety-four times more likely to die from being run over by a texting driver, from heart disease, cancer, liver failure, suicide, or AIDS—than by murder.

The hidden knife. The strangers swarming. The ice floes on the river like an invitation to a crazed and likely fatal game of hopscotch. None of these would you be able to truly see were you not drifting on foot with open eyes.

# What Happens at the Woodward

### AARON FOLEY

from **Sweeter Voices Still: An LGBTQ Anthology from Middle America**

A former coworker of mine posted a photo of herself on Facebook with a bruised, swollen eye, and cuts on her face still fresh. Shortly after came another status saying she had been hit in the face with a bottle during a fight. And then after that, another status saying that it had happened at the Woodward and, according to her, the staff had not been helpful when she lodged a complaint.

How a cisgender, heterosexual woman got caught in a bar fight at a gay bar should be a mystery, but not in Detroit. She had posted that others had told her about the Woodward, and "that's what happens there." Those folks, unfortunately, are right. That is how it is at the Woodward Cocktail Bar, located at the intersection of Grand Boulevard—we call it "the boulevard"—and Woodward Avenue just a few miles north of now-bustling downtown Detroit.

As a Black gay man, the Woodward, which largely caters to men (and once a week, women) like me, is supposed to be my scene. I've been gay-clubbing and bar-hopping in New York City, Chicago, San Francisco, even as far away as Milan and Melbourne, and there's no place quite like home. (Well, except maybe Atlanta.) I resist the word "urban" at all costs when it comes to describing anything Black. It's what the bar is described as when compared to other gay bars in Metro Detroit that play Top Forty music. The Woodward plays hip-hop and R&B, and not just the generics. It plays eastside Detroit hood shit, hustle—a very specific Detroit-style brand of line dancing, trap, jit, baby-making jams from ten years ago that still sizzle, and, on specific days, old school from way back in the day. There are no dance remixes of Adele. There are house remixes of Kelly Price.

It is the hub for Detroit's Black gays, and perhaps the last time a white gay was there—except for the charming Russian behind the bar—

was when, on a whim, I brought along the one I was dating at the time. (People stared at us crazy, by the way—my bad.) The drinks, despite being made with liquors found anywhere, are unusually strong and have reached mythical status in their city—never more than two if you want to make it out alive. And speaking of the bar, it famously only takes cash, even in the age of Square and other such money-exchange methods. The younger gays are on the dance floor in one room, while the older gays are in the front room at the bar. All ages can be found smoking weed on the patio.

I've flirted here, and hooked up later, as a single man. One of my exes flirted here, and likely hooked up later now that I think about it, while we were together. I once ran into his cousin here coked out of his mind. I've ran into guys who, like me, were closeted in high school. I would see regulars here for years who'd turn up dead later, announced via Facebook. While working in the mayor's office of Detroit, I brought our very-recognizable-in-the-public-eye chief of staff here for the first time. Another coworker I took for the first time learned the hard way about what happens after two drinks. Everyone's got a Woodward story about the good times. Everyone's also got a story about the time they had to evacuate the club because of a fight, got caught in the middle of a melee in progress or the stampede out, or, once in my case and more than once in many others', dodged bullets from gunfire outside.

We've got a culture of violence at the Woodward that everyone's quietly accepted since, well, as long as I can remember. It's not like it happens every single night. It doesn't. But there's always the risk of a fight breaking out on the dance floor—or in one of the parking lots—over some dumb shit. "He was looking at my man." "He stepped on my shoe." "He think he cute." "He owes me money." There's never a good reason. It's just how it is. It may be the strong-as-hell drinks. It may be because we're from Detroit, a city that, for all its greatness, has been mired in violence for as long as anybody, young or old, at the club has been alive. It may be petty gay drama. But whether we accept it or not, our relationship with the Woodward is complicated.

I think about where the Woodward fits into Detroit's larger story a lot. As a majority Black city where, for decades, a significant part of that population has lived in poverty, it can sometimes be survival of the fittest. You have no choice but to be forgiving of people who have always been disenfranchised and put into circumstances out of their control. If Black Americans have always had the short end of the stick during our time in this country, many Detroiters have had nothing at all to grasp on to. So we fight, physically. We grow up knowing how to fight for our lives, and in the case of many gay men, perhaps knowing how to fight for that before having to defend yourself against someone calling you a fag. It's just the way it's been in Detroit, and that carries over to the Woodward.

I don't think, however, the Woodward has kept up with the change in LGBTQ culture around it. At a time when the community has moved more toward community in the face of adversity, even if that community is, frankly, still fractured along racial lines, it seems more and more that the Woodward prides itself on being reflective of Detroit and only Detroit—to a fault. So much of a fault that we just look away from the fights and come back the next weekend. Except now, Detroit feels like it's moving on, seeing a resurgence after years of decline. And there's a larger conversation about the changing demographics of the city that's happening alongside this renewal.

For all its faults, the Woodward is very much Old Detroit. People have never fought at the new gay bar downtown by the RenCen, the first new gay bar to open in the city—and actually last for more than a year—in more than a decade. But that bar is also very downtown, and often very white. There's something nostalgic about a bar that only takes cash when everywhere else is striving toward Apple Pay, but in a city where many people may not even have the means to open a bank account, it somehow feels accessible. Another gay male coworker of mine notes the history of the pre-fighting Woodward, about how back in the eighties and well into the nineties, it was a space where the kinds of house music that Madonna and other musicians would take mainstream first flourished, and how that history should be preserved in the face of gentrification, which may or may not be, depending on who you talk to, rapidly moving in the Woodward's direction.

The Woodward sits at the end of the QLine, a much-derided light rail that runs 3.3 miles in each direction from the center of downtown to the edge of New Center where the bar is. Despite many criticisms of the train itself—it's slow, it malfunctions, it's generally faster to take a bus, ride a scooter, or even walk—the property values along the route have risen. More new housing and retail are being built along Woodward. The old coney island across the street, from where those bullets I once dodged flew out when a guy fired his gun at another guy and broke the plate glass window, has closed. There are more white people in New Center than I've ever seen. People still pack the Woodward night after night. But a common horror story in Detroit is longtime businesses shuttering or changing identity when a landlord buys out, or prices out, a tenant. I tried to contact the owner or a manager of the Woodward to find out where they stand, but getting a hold of that information is a challenge. Half the time someone might pick up the phone, half the time they'd say call back another time. But then, I think about the fights.

Sometimes people say to keep Detroit as Old Detroit is to keep as many elements of Old Detroit there as possible—including our violence. I've joked on Twitter, the same way people told my old coworker who got her eye busted open, that there's always a fight at the Woodward. Part of that is self-deprecation as a member of Detroit's turbulent Black LGBTQ community. But another part of that is defense, in a weird way. What would Detroit be without the Woodward? Would this place become another stale top forty gay bar that, like that infamous one in Chicago and probably everywhere else, explicitly bans hip-hop as a subtle way to keep the Black people out? Would it even be a gay bar at all and just become another overpriced cocktail bar with drinks made with fresh herbs, Japanese whiskeys, and revived spirits du jour? Do we, or I, worry too much about the fights because of what the white people might think? Like, "Oh, look at those thugs fighting again, that's so Detroit." Or should we keep the Woodward as is, fists and all, as defiance against the white gaze?

It's complicated, just like Detroit is complicated. So I guess this is what we'll have to do in the meantime, which is what I've always done. When you go, don't leave your mind vulnerable to bad decisions by drinking too much. Keep an eye for the exits, and know when to make an exit. Stay behind the brick wall that backs the old hardware store next door if you hear gunshots. But, I guess, always have fun. I never mean to put the Woodward down. I've had way more good times there than bad, and I'd wager we can all say the same. That's just what happens there.

# The Pennsylvania I Carry with Me

## ANNIE MAROON

from **Red State Blues: Stories from Midwestern Life on the Left**

Five years after I left, I got Pennsylvania inked into my skin. It was my second autumn post-college, and the notion that I might never live in my home state again was sinking in. So I decided to carry the state outline on my left shoulder, with the major rivers of the western third, where I grew up, drawn in blue.

I knew by junior high that I would leave Greensburg as soon as I was old enough. Both of my parents left the states where they grew up by their early twenties. My mom left Ohio for New Orleans, and my dad departed West Virginia for North Carolina. (Both eventually circled back to Pittsburgh; that part of the arc is only now beginning to seem relevant to me.)

At eighteen, I chose Boston. I almost never got homesick in college. That came later, once I became what you'd call a permanent resident of Massachusetts rather than a college kid. I spent a summer in western Massachusetts thinking about the mountains and creeks I grew up with, thinking about a cockeyed, hilly city where three rivers intersect, crossed by iconic bridges. I missed the geography, and I missed the people. My brother and I had left, but almost my entire extended family lives within a few hours of Pittsburgh.

And I thought a lot about the realization that hit me when I was seventeen and about to leave: that I would always be shaped by this place. I could roll my eyes and despair over the people around me in my rural-suburban county who never seemed to want to travel farther away than Pittsburgh. I could cast around for something fun to do with friends and wind up at the mall or the twenty-four-hour Eat 'n' Park, because there was nothing else. But all that was part of me. I never wanted to get so far from home, mentally, that I forgot that.

Some states are iconic. Their names and shapes are evocative, synonymous with a way of life. Pennsylvania doesn't have that. It's a big state but not big enough to have the outsized fantasies attached to it that California, Texas, or even Alaska have. It has major cities, but no New York or Chicago or Los Angeles. It's a perpetual swing state, voting Democratic in presidential elections all my life (until 2016), but never overwhelmingly enough to gain a reputation for it. People sometimes see the western part of my tattoo and ask if it's Massachusetts, mistaking the Allegheny River for the Connecticut. Others have squinted at it, running through the middle of the country in their minds: *Ohio? Colorado?* In college, most of the real East Coast kids thought I lived somewhere in the suburbs of Philadelphia. Westmoreland County isn't flyover country the way that, say, Nebraska is. From my parents' house, you can drive to DC in four hours, New York City in six. But I learned the term "Pennsyltucky" early to describe my homeland (long before *Orange Is the New Black* used it for a character who, in the show, isn't even from Pennsylvania, but Virginia). The term is a little too easy—dismissive of Kentucky as well as a huge swath of Pennsylvania—but while it irks me coming from New Englanders, I forgive it coming from others who grew up there.

The first election I really experienced was 2000. I was nine years old, in fourth grade, and it was the first time I realized just how different my family was from the families of my classmates. Kids talked, in the way kids do, about how they would vote for George W. Bush because their parents were. In my fourth-grade class of about twenty-five kids, only two of us—my friend Marissa and I—were in Al Gore's camp. (One other boy implied that he might have been with us, but he didn't exactly want to stick his neck out. He and I are Facebook friends now, which means I see his pro-Trump posts.)

That was it: Marissa and I, taking whatever insults a bunch of vaguely conservative fourth graders could hurl at us. We snapped back at our classmates pretty well, as I remember it, and the election went on for a month. At the end of it, George Bush was president, and I felt somehow separate from the kid who had entered the school year, terrified of having anyone pay attention to her. I was different, and now everybody knew it.

In eighth grade, my mother took me to a rally in downtown Greensburg before the 2004 election, where I hollered across the street at a friend's father, who was waving an inflatable dolphin to mock John Kerry's "flip-flopping." I absorbed my parents' lukewarm acceptance of the Democratic nominee and wore a Kerry button to school on Election Day. It was still pretty much just Marissa and me, but I was settling into my identity as one of Latrobe Junior High's token lefties.

The summer before senior year, I spent two weeks at journalism camp in Washington, DC, with kids from all over the country. I made friends from New Jersey and Los Angeles and Queens, all of whom were astounded when we watched the documentary *Outfoxed*. Okay, but nobody really *believes* what's on Fox News, they said. Nobody actually *watches* that stuff and thinks it's true.

I remember exchanging looks with a girl from Tennessee. We tried to explain that, well, yeah, some people—including people we love— *do* watch Fox News, and they do think it's the best place to get their information. We disagree with them, but we love them and want them to be safe and healthy and happy. Sometimes we're alarmed by the things that come out of their mouths, though, and the violence with which those things come out.

I don't know if it is better or worse to grow up in a place that does not share most of your values. I do know that it forces you to see people who are different from you as human, rather than as some faceless concept (like the mythic, monolithic "white working class," or the occupants of something called "Trump Country"). They are your day-to-day life, the people you joke with on the afternoon bus and the people who sit by you in class. Sometimes you settle for rolling your eyes when they talk politics, because arguing with them is too exhausting. In rare triumphant moments, you stand up to a smarmy Republican teacher who takes for granted that everyone agrees with him, or at least that everyone will shut up and pretend they agree with him.

Since November 2016, "empathy" has become a loaded word. Empathy is something western Pennsylvania taught me. As a writer, empathy is something I can't help and can't afford to lose; I want to understand other people. Flat characters are for formulaic superhero movies with good guys and bad guys, not the stories I want to tell.

But empathy does not mean a free pass. My empathy for your real pain and hardship doesn't get you off the hook for deciding that a candidate's racism, xenophobia, and misogyny weren't that big of a deal because you didn't think they'd affect you directly, or just didn't think they mattered that much. And nothing rings more hollow than a think piece pleading with the people in the line of fire—Black folks, Latin folks, immigrants, queer and trans people, Muslims, women, Jewish people, people who need Medicaid for life-saving services—to empathize with those who put them there. Why should they be obligated to peer into the souls of people who couldn't be bothered to do the same for them?

In the summer of 2016, I drove from Massachusetts to Greensburg. The last leg of the journey took me from featureless, gray Route 22 onto Route 119, through little towns like Crabtree and the rolling green fields that signal home to me. I used to get lost on purpose in these hills coming back from college, soaking in the scenery. This time, every pocket of civilization I passed was scattered with Trump signs, like clusters of fungus on fallen trees. This wasn't surprising; after voting twice for Bill Clinton, my county had gone Republican since 2000. I have always known who my neighbors are. But I felt sick in a way I hadn't felt about the John McCain signs that sprouted all over my hometown in 2008. I might have rolled my eyes or sighed, at McCain and Mitt Romney, but I did not feel afraid at the sight of them.

On election night, I watched the results with my colleagues at our office in Springfield, Massachusetts. I didn't leave until Pennsylvania had been called, around 1:40 a.m. The next morning, I began sorting through my emotions. I considered the facts. In total, just about six million people, half the population of Pennsylvania, had voted at all. The winning candidate's margin of victory was narrow, not even a majority—just less than 49 percent of the vote to just less than 48. I knew all this, but still I felt, that morning, betrayed by my own skin.

But I am proud of what western Pennsylvania made me. I am proud of my mother, who took me to ragtag protests throughout my youth, who is so vocally opposed to this administration that acquaintances and friends often send her private messages on Facebook, thanking her for saying things they aren't bold enough to say themselves. I am proud of my father, who provides medical care to kids in the poor, rural areas that voted hard for Trump, the areas in desperate need of help from someone who cares about them outside of an election cycle. I am proud of my friends and relatives who still live there, and of all the members of the community who do the crucial, unglamorous work of making people's lives better.

What was killing me November 9, 2016, was the small, irrational hope I'd held that the people who sat next to me at my brother's hockey games, drove me to and from practices, and came to my graduation party would be decent enough to look at Donald Trump and say, enough is enough. Yes, we are conservative, we are Republicans, but some things matter more than party lines, and this is not a normal Republican presidential candidate.

Some of them were decent enough, of course. But a lot of them were not. And the people of whom I'm thinking are not all members of that much-scrutinized white working class with all of their economic anxiety. They are all white, yes, but many live quite comfortably. Their cars are large, with trunks big enough to carry multiple hockey bags, and their spacious homes sit in immaculate housing developments. Some are old classmates who, in the culture vacuum of the suburbs, embraced a certain "redneck" identity that celebrated their realness, their true American-ness, which they demonstrate largely through drinking at country concerts.

I don't know whether their feelings are changing now that white supremacists feel comfortable enough to openly display their colors all around the country, some of them saying outright that this administration has emboldened them to do so. I have stayed Facebook friends with some acquaintances from the area; there are times to unfriend and unfollow, but I am afraid of what happens if we all cut ourselves off completely from people with whom we disagree. One woman, who posted in November that she voted for the president based on his position on abortion, voiced disappointment and a sense of betrayal in August, in the days after Charlottesville. I haven't heard much from anyone else.

Three years ago, when I got my tattoo, I figured the odds were better than not that I would never live in Pennsylvania again. Kids like me flee towns like mine all over the country, for all sorts of good reasons, and a lot of them don't come back. My county lost more population between 2010 and 2016 than any other county in Pennsylvania. Some people leave seeking jobs. Others leave seeking safer places that will fit them better or threaten them less; my queer friends from home left for bigger cities. I left in part because I wanted to explore a new place, to start over in a city where nobody knew me. Somewhere along the line, I put down tentative roots; the hills and old mountains in the northwest part of my adopted state have been a good enough facsimile of home. The fall of 2018 will mark my tenth in Massachusetts.

But now I can see myself in Pittsburgh. Maybe in a year, maybe further off, but I can imagine it. Maybe if I want to keep talking up my unromantic swing state, I need to put my money where my mouth is. There are people in western Pennsylvania, and in Ohio and West Virginia, who deserve better than a president who will play to their fears and anxieties in election season and strive to leave them without health care months later. They deserve someone who will speak honestly about how we got this way and provide real solutions, rather than taking the cowardly cop-out of casting immigrants and people of color as convenient enemies.

But maybe it is too easy for me to give a rousing speech from western Massachusetts, where Bernie Sanders dominated the bumper-sticker race from the start and won my town's primary vote with ease. The week before Christmas in 2016, my brother and I were driving home through the center of the state—the white-hot core of Pennsyltucky, if you must—under an astonishing pink sunset that stayed with us as we wound west, past barns in picturesque fields covered with snow.

I tried not to think about politics. I wanted to fight for the land and sky themselves, to protect them somehow from harm. It is easy to romanticize from the highway, and easy to dismiss or speak grandly, from hundreds of miles away. That day it was hard, maybe impossible, to hold everything I felt about Pennsylvania in my heart at the same time.

# Flex Cleveland

## ERIK PIEPENBURG

from **Midwest Architecture Journeys**

The Cleveland skyline is like an old-school gay porn star. Butch. Firm. Solid. A top.

Watching over Public Square like an eagle-eyed Secret Service agent is the Terminal Tower, the city's fifty-two-story signature skyscraper, designed by Graham, Anderson, Probst, and White. On the shore of Lake Erie, like a geek-punk Poseidon, stands I. M. Pei's geometric record player for the Rock and Roll Hall of Fame. Ameritrust Tower, the Marcel Breuer and Hamilton Smith building at East Ninth Street and Euclid Avenue, doesn't give a damn what you think about its rigid brutalism. It's now part of a swank hotel and residential complex called the 9.

Then there's the building at 2600 Hamilton Avenue, a sturdy architectural gem planted firmly on the ground like a guard dog. It's a living throwback to Cleveland's industrial, working-man roots that also happens to be the biggest gay sex club in the world.

## I. Sex and Much More

Walled off from a sleepy, industrial neighborhood just east of downtown is Flex, part of a nationwide chain of twenty-four-hour bathhouses. For the uninitiated, that means it's a private club where men go to socialize and have sex with each other.

It offers the usual bathhouse amenities: a pool, a well-stocked gym, a rotating calendar of porn star appearances, and private cabanas and open public areas for sex. But unlike other bathhouses around the world, Flex is massive. With over fifty thousand square feet, it even has a hotel, where a presidential suite goes for $219 a night, far pricier than some traditional hotel rooms in town. Since opening in 2006, Flex has become a destination; one travel writer called it "a virtual monument to gay bathhouse culture."

(A previous incarnation of the bathhouse was located downtown in a much smaller space at West Ninth and St. Clair.)

I've been to Flex a few times. On the first visit, I remember being shocked at its size. Once you pay your admission and check in, you put on your towel—standard bathhouse attire—and enter the wet area. There's a huge pool, multiman jacuzzi, DJ booth (music is always playing), shower area, and a steam room maze. It was only after I walked past the large gym that I realized I'd only seen half the space. I pushed through a door and found rows of hotel rooms and a kitchen where you could order food from a smiling chef. I remember catfish on the menu one Friday night.

The second floor is all about sex: There's sex in rooms, through gloryholes, on slings, and out in the open. But there is also a library-style room where you can sit and watch a movie or socialize. A roof deck lets you check out the Cleveland skyline or hobnob with a visiting porn star shooting a video to be shared on Flex's Twitter feed.

Walk around and you'll marvel at how the curved edges, horizontal lines, and street-level windows look far more Miami Beach than Cleveland. It's only when you start looking into the history of the building that you realize what a pedigreed architectural history the Flex building has.

## II. A New Style

Many of Flex's structural elements are unchanged from its opening in 1939, when it was born as a Greyhound bus office and garage that introduced Cleveland to the style known as Streamline Moderne, a child of art deco characterized by nautical elements like curved corners, glass block walls, and smooth finishes. Buildings are usually rendered in aquamarine, turquoise and other colors that reference the ocean. The overall effect gives buildings a sleek, bursting-forth feeling, like a boat surging confidently on water. There are Streamline Moderne sewing machines and radios but also diners, motels, and bus terminals.

From the street, Flex catches the eye with hallmarks of Streamline Moderne, like the rounded facade, ultramarine tiles, oversized windows, and dramatic horizontal lines that run the length of the building. The original industrial purpose of the building makes the small artistic flourishes in the architecture more meaningful.

To really understand Streamline Moderne's place in Cleveland requires a visit to the extraordinary Greyhound terminal at East Fourteenth Street and Chester Avenue, designed by the architect W. S. Arrasmith. In a 2015 feature in Cleveland's *Plain Dealer*, the reporter Alison Grant interviewed Frank Wrenick, the author of the book *The Streamline Era Greyhound Terminals*, who said the 250-foot-long facility was described by the *Cleveland News* as "the greatest bus terminal in the world" when it opened in 1948. The building was added to the National Register of Historic Places in 1999 and remains a Greyhound bus terminal.

It's obvious why Streamline Moderne came to Cleveland in the 1930s and 1940s. The style is associated with the locomotive design and industrial production of the period, elements strongly associated with Cleveland's past. Streamline Moderne emerged like a "path to a new day," as the Cleveland architect David Ellison told me over the phone.

"Trains and fast travel were glorified in the late twenties and the thirties," said Ellison. "After World War I, Cleveland had it with the old-fashioned stuff. Everybody was trying something new."

## III. "A Place to Visit"

I tried to get in touch with the management at Flex to find out more about the renovation, but I never heard back from anyone. Maybe talking about the architectural significance of the place wasn't in keeping with the Flex brand. So I reached out to Michelle Jarboe, the crackerjack real estate reporter for the *Plain Dealer* who knows how to find out anything about any building in the city. It took her almost no time to get some fascinating documentation of Flex's former life. According to maps dated from the late 1920s through the 1930s, the entire block was Greyhound. A fire insurance map shows garages with room for over forty coaches, work pits, and washing and servicing stations. There are records of property transfers between various Greyhound entities for decades.

The man behind Flex was Charles R. Fleck, an activist and philanthropist who founded the Flex chain. A Cleveland native who died in 2012 at seventy-three, Fleck was interested in making bathhouses more than just buildings where men could have sex. Todd Saporito, who runs the Flex franchise, said in Fleck's obituary in the *Gay People's Chronicle*, a now-shuttered Cleveland gay newspaper, that Fleck wanted Flex to be a venue where "everyone had a place to visit, even though they may have been disowned from family and friends."

According to a 2006 article in *Cleveland Scene*, an alternative weekly, Fleck spent $1.2 million on the three-acre property, with $6 million going toward building renovations. Fleck faced opposition from some public health officials in town who were worried that a bathhouse would lead to an increase in unsafe sex. Fleck told the local NPR station that Flex will "probably hand out and give away and purchase more condoms than anybody in the world."

## IV. A Queer Space

Why is Flex's Streamline Moderne past so fascinating to me? Because it's old and new and queer and naughty and under the radar and so many more things that I value as a gay man. It's also a piece of gay history. After Stonewall, gay bathhouses became wildly popular with a gay community that was desperate for sexual connection in a shared sexual space. The places were gritty, for sure, but many were also majestic. The Continental Baths in New York was located in the basement of the landmark Ansonia Hotel. But the AIDS epidemic forced the closure of many gay bathhouses, eventually leaving those that remained or reopened to move into cramped and completely unremarkable spaces.

The eye-catching architecture of Flex aggrandizes, whether you think it should or not, the idea that what's happening inside is valuable, treasured, and special. The difference between going to Flex and any other bathhouse is the difference between seeing a movie at a suburban multiplex or at a restored vaudeville-era theater in Cleveland's landmark Playhouse Square. Think of it this way: Traveling to and from the mighty Grand Central Station in New York makes you and your trip feel important. To and from Penn Station, not so much. One is meaningful; the other is utilitarian.

If I ran Flex, I'd promote the hell out of the building's ancestry. I'd do so with the same pride as does Heinen's, the downtown grocery store that opened in 2015 inside a magnificently renovated 1908 bank on Euclid Avenue that was originally designed by George Browne Post, the architect behind the New York Stock Exchange.

I would also make sure that every gay man in the world knew about it. Flex—and in turn Cleveland itself—is losing out on the gay tourist dollar by not advertising itself as a one-of-a-kind-gay experience. Whether or not you visit to hook up, a trip to Flex is a chance to experience the gay past in a way that's authentic, nostalgic, and entertaining.

I could even see taking a walking tour of the place. Towel required.

# 79

## BRIAN BROOME

### from The Pittsburgh Neighborhood Guidebook

The very last 79 East Hills bus leaves Wilkinsburg Station at exactly 12:15 a.m. on weeknights, and I am usually the last one on it by the time it reaches Park Hill Drive, where I live. Not many people walk my neighborhood after dark. It is usually me, having gotten off a late shift at work, and the irritated bus driver sitting in silence underneath the flickering fluorescent light that sucks up any real light, blanching everything until it is an odd shade of greenish blue. The street is dark apart from the headlights of the bus, and the ramshackle houses are set a bit back from the road where trees overhang. It would be charming were it not so ugly; the houses crammed up against one another like brown teeth. Poor makes everything ugly. The both of us, the bus driver and I, are silently impatient to be back in our normally lit homes and can just about taste freedom. But tonight, our quiet time is interrupted by a rumbling in the distance; a communal shouting that grows louder and louder as the bus creeps slowly up Park Hill Drive, and when the noise reaches its peak, we were set upon by a horde of drunken children who come out of nowhere like native warriors shrieking out battle cries. Illuminated only by public chariot headlights; shouting and banging at the sides of the bus seemingly to attempt with all their energy to rock it off its wheels and overturn it with me and a terrified white man inside. He leans on the horn, but it does not deter them. As with most miscreants, it only serves to incite them and fuel the attack to a fever pitch. I can smell liquor through the bus walls and the scent of marijuana far more pungent than the usual dusting of it that always hangs in the air around these parts. I briefly wonder where their parents are, as if that would do anything to stem the tide of this ocean of howling Black, bloodthirsty faces bent on the wreaking of havoc; this insanity. I can only assume my death is imminent. The driver is now frantically fumbling for his radio as it crackles and sputters with the sounds of truncated words as he tries to explain what's happening to some incredulous and disembodied voice.

And then, as quickly as it started, it is over. The whoops and hollers that proceeded the attack fade off into the distance. The excitement couldn't have lasted more than a minute or so but felt like an eternity, and he and I quietly creep up the road, where the bus heaves a sigh of relief and spits me out.

We are both as silent as we'd started out. He just pulls away noisily, leaving me alone under a streetlamp until I can hear crickets. Welcome to the East Hills neighborhood of Pittsburgh, where we proudly display the Seven.

## Gluttony

"For the drunkard and the glutton will come to poverty, and slumber will clothe them with rags." (Proverbs 23:21)

If you offer me a drink, you'll almost immediately regret it. I can guarantee it. When I imbibe, it's an all-day affair and into the night until my body can't take anymore. I will vomit on my shoes and start all over again. I won't stop until someone pries the bottle from my hand and locks me up. I love alcohol and would bathe in it given half a chance. Were I to have my druthers, I would completely bypass the circuitous route of my mouth and inject it directly into my bloodstream so that it could perform its magical workings with even more expeditious mercy. In my fantasies, every vending machine is stocked with deliciously brown liquors and little baggies full of granular white goodies, and there is one on every street corner. In short, I am an addict. I am the innocent victim of an extended adolescence and an arrested development. I have drunk and drugged so much so as not to remember my own name on some nights, wake up in agonizing pain, and do it all again the next day and the next. I am a glutton for punishment. But, firstly and most importantly, a glutton for intoxicants of all kinds. This is why I live here.

A life lived in avoidance of reality is expensive, and the East Hills falls perfectly within my price range. I am here because I have drank my opportunities in life. I have drank away a good job. I have drugged away my vacations, and I have snorted my future. I have filled myself to bursting with pharmaceutical delusion, and my punishment for all that fun is to live here, where all Seven of them are on display daily. I have sacrificed the privilege of living in the nicer neighborhoods in the city. I live where I can afford. But unlike these people, I don't belong here. I am literate. I have merely and temporarily lost my way, but I will recover. This ghetto element around here would never understand that here is a mere transitory stop for me; a blip on my radar. This is why they don't talk to me. I have made no friends here because I am bound for greater things someday, and they all know it. They can smell it on me. I live here only because it is what I can afford; not because I am part of this cannabis scented Bedlam where the residents talk about doing time in jail the way normal people discuss going to the grocery store. The problem with being a glutton is that there is always a price to pay in the end. Dues. For me, the East Hills of Pittsburgh is dues.

## Pride

"Pride goeth before destruction and a haughty spirit before a fall." (Proverbs 16:18)

I live at caruncle of the Eye of Horus. On a map, you can see how the streets Park Hill Drive and East Hills Drive form an almost perfect Eye of Horus; a noose. I stand at the corner every day waiting for the 79. It's a convolution bus that goes round and round the rim of the Eye of Horus over and over again, ferrying miscreants from one meaningless errand to another. The public housing complex is situated right in the pupil. Whoever built them this time made sure to make them colorful. The units are painted purple and blue and red in some sort of attempt to make them cheerful but resulting in what looks to me like a dysfunctional Gingerbread Land sitting atop a hill. The 79 circles the perimeter all day long. Round and round all day, so much like water in a toilet bowl that won't properly flush.

My shoe has a hole in the sole today. I have no umbrella, and the rain has gotten into and has dampened my sock. As I look up from this minor annoyance, I notice that today, she is wearing red. She is the woman who shoots me scornful looks and drives a car that shines silver like new sixpence. It positively gleams. I don't know what kind of car it is, but it doesn't belong here. It should belong to a celebrity or someone that I was told I should aspire to be; like a doctor or a lawyer. Its luxury belongs to a woman who stops by to visit my neighbor a few times a week. She parks it right in front of the bus stop, obstructing my access to its utilitarian comforts when it finally arrives, and today, her vehicle smells of coconut air freshener and an expensive flower-based perfume. She emerges haughty and well dressed and, as the door opens, the rhythmic thump from rap music that was muffled before booms at top volume from her pimped-out ride. She is in a red dress and high heels. I smile at her, but no return smile is offered. Instead, she fixes me with elevator eyes that start at the top floor of my nappy hair and end at my now waterlogged basement of a shoe with the sock growing soggier and slimier by the second. She moves past me wordlessly and lofty, throwing an expensive shawl over her shoulder in a grandiose motion. I am in no position to be acknowledged whatsoever. She greets my neighbor, and they proceed with some sort of hushed business inside his home before she emerges triumphant to, once again, climb behind the wheel of her blinding blingwagon and speed off only to park its majesty in the ramshackle driveway of the ramshackle apartment that she lives in a mere five ramshackle houses up the road. She lives here too. It will never cease to amaze me what great pains people who live in this ghetto will go to in order to try to make it appear as if they don't live in this ghetto. The dilapidated home to fancy car ratio is unacceptable, and the combined cost of sneakers and clothes people from this neighborhood buy could most likely settle the national debt with change left over.

The issue of pride in the East Hills is one that is complicated. And money is utilized not for what it can do for you in reality but for how it can make you look in the eyes of others and in your own deluded mind. The bill of goods that's been sold around here is thoroughly on display in the form if intricate hairdos whose upkeep make it impossible to pay electric bills on time, and the ridiculously expensive bottles of liquor at the conveniently located liquors purveyor (right next to the Dollar Store) that eat into the grocery budget. It's the kind of liquor that the rappers drink. You are what you wear and drink and drive and I, with my soaking wet sock and rain-dripping forehead, will not fall prey to it. I won't live up to the stereotype and be trapped here in a state of perpetual adolescence. It's a modest life that is the key to success, and I won't forget that. The issue of pride in this ghetto is the issue that keeps people struggling. One must learn to adjust to one's circumstances. If they would only learn how to live within their means, all things would be possible. I narrow my eyes and take solace in the fact that the Lady in Red's fancy car will be taken away from her one day owing to her irresponsibility. Repossessed. Someday, I will see her on the 79, and I'll just politely nod in such a way so that she knows that I know that I've recognized her fall from ersatz grace and that she should have known better. It is my humble and modest nature that will one day lift me out of this place. Slow and steady wins the race.

## Sloth

"Through sloth the roof sinks in, and through indolence the house leaks." (Ecclesiastes 10:18)

My doorbell is ringing at 8:00 a.m. on a Sunday morning, and, before I even open my eyes, I already know who it is. He will keep ringing it until I get up to answer, so it's best to just get it over with right now. My vision is blurry and my body is heavy with sleepiness. I throw on an old bathrobe and lumber down the stairs, holding on to the railing for dear life before I close one eye to look through the peephole. Face distorted through the tiny funhouse mirror glass and eyes popped out and run through with blood red spider webs. Thin as a rail and swallowed up in dirty clothes. He is sorry, and I can feel his shame through the door before I even open it and, when I do, the cold blast of stale, sickly sweet liquor smell almost knocks me over, carried by the chilly morning wind.

"I am so sorry, sir."

As we stand there and I close my dirty bathrobe around my neck, I know that these are the words he'll lead with. Jody has never called me anything but "sir" even though he is easily a decade older than me. His eyes are wet either with the cold or with the sting of being hungover. He is sorry, but he does not remember fully what happened last night; only the flashing of police lights in the wee hours and that men in blue uniforms came to his house. As we stand there, both shivering, I take the opportunity to refresh his memory of the previous evening. Jody, next-door neighbor and indolent drunk.

I spent most of last evening on my knees in my bed banging on the wall that separates our bedrooms. The walls around here are rice paper, and whatever your neighbor does on his side may as well be done right in front of you. But even if they were constructed from kryptonite, you could still hear Jody's insanity clear as a cannon shot. Like me, Jody is a drunk, although a far less responsible one. I work for a living. But Jody cannot be bothered to take up such intrusions. The bottle requires all of his time, and I take this opportunity to not invite him in, allow him to shiver on my doorstep, and recount every detail of his antics since I've been unfortunate enough to come to this place. He braces for the onslaught; head bowed, unable to meet my seething gaze. I am furious with lack of sleep and we've been here before.

Last night, Jody, you began your screaming through the walls at ghosts and, as you stand here in the clothes that you've been wearing for a week, I need to once again, fill in your memory as you cover your face and feign remorse. You are like every other no-good, do-nothing drunk in this neighborhood, and, underneath it all, I can tell that you are perfectly healthy. Able-bodied. I tell him proudly that I was the one who called the police, and he whimpers with shame and his voice cracks out an "I'm so sorry, sir."

The fact of the matter is that no one visits you and you have no family because you cannot be bothered to get your act together, Jody. Your life is just one long comfortable nap on the couch while your surroundings fall to pieces. I have seen you day in and day out, sitting and staring into space in the driver's seat of that stationary junk heap you call a car all day long, getting drunk, and then I have to deal with the fallout. You shout at invisible phantoms all night long, and, last night, you took the show on the road out to our shared courtyard, screaming for all you're worth and punching at the air. Your awkward and drunken jujitsu was on full display for a private audience of me at three o'clock in the morning. I watched you through the window performing your clumsy kicks into the stratosphere, fighting and shouting at an invisible attacker and falling over backward. Your pathetic attempts to recover leaving you rolling around on your back like an overturned turtle. It was the most movement I've ever seen out of you, Jody. So, I called the police. They came again to laugh at you openly and try to coax you back into the house stumbling, only for it to start up all over again twenty minutes later. I will call the police every time, even though no one else around here seems to be willing to for some reason. But I will call them. Every night.

He still has not met my eyes. When he finally opens his mouth to speak again, I am foolishly waiting to hear something new come from his lips. But he just stammers and, in a voice as brittle as kindling, mumbles out yet another "I'm so sorry, sir." His breath cuts through the cold and causes vomit to hitch in my throat, and I can tell that he's already thinking about his precious liquor to smooth over the rough edges of my harsh words. He embodies the work ethic around here. He inebriates himself to the point of dementia and thinks that the world owes him something. This is who he screams at every night through the walls. I'm sure of it. He is fighting the world

Through sickeningly sweet liquor breath and a hung head, Jody tells me that he'll never do it again and turns slowly to walk, not to his house but to his car through the snow. I tell him that he might want to look into getting a job. He walks to the weird purple vehicle and gets inside, where he'll sit in lethargy all day long trying to change reality by looking at it through the bottom of a bottle. I have work in a few hours, so I march back upstairs triumphant to try to get some much deserved sleep. I will fail. Because as Jody and I both know, there is truly no rest for the weary.

## Envy

"I have seen the fool taking root, but suddenly I cursed his dwelling."
(Job 5:3)

### Community Crime Update: 10/4/2015 Burglary/Aggravated Assault: 2400 Block of Bracey Drive, 7:30 a.m.

A thirty-six-year-old female victim reported that a known suspect, S. D. Kelley, thirty-seven, of East Pittsburgh, broke into her house by forcing open the front door. The suspect then stole a frozen chicken. Then Ms. Kelley pulled out a knife and began swinging it at the victim like a woman possessed. Officers arrived on scene and detained Ms. Kelley, who they found out in front of the residence shouting. The frozen chicken was located roosting in her purse. Kelley told officers that she and the victim were both romantically involved with the same man. While officers were attempting to get the full and ridiculous story from this ostensibly grown woman, a male, M. Henderson, thirty-seven, of East Hills, emerged from the residence and tried to interfere with the arrest. Mr. Henderson shoved Officer Pucci and then took a swing at Officer McManaway. Witnessing this, Officer Welling deployed his Taser, shocking the shit out of M. Henderson, which immediately stopped his assault. M. Henderson was then also taken into custody. Both suspects were then taken to the Allegheny County Jail. Ms. Kelley was charged with burglary and simple assault, while Mr. Henderson was charged with obstructing the administration of law and aggravated assault. When queried, neighbors chalked this incident up to just another in the daily recurrence of supposedly grown women fighting for the attentions of a no-account man, as romantic entanglement and drama are the only things that people with no education, no future, and no prospects ever spend their time on. Jealous and possessive behavior is what passes for romantic love in poor neighborhoods. But many people in the neighborhood remain confused as to why a person would retaliate against a romantic rival by breaking into her house and stealing a frozen chicken. All have dismissed the event as just another in a series of ghetto dramas that make the neighborhood look foolish on local television. One neighbor (standing at the bus stop with a hole in his shoe and suffering from obvious sleep deprivation) who wished to remain anonymous, rolled his eyes at the news of another domestic occurrence citing that, "It happens every day because these people around here have nothing better to do." At the time of this printing, the whereabouts of the frozen chicken are unknown.

## Lust

"They have become callous and have given themselves up to sensuality, to practice every kind of impurity." (Ephesians 4:19)

Never in all my born days have I seen so many little babies slung over the hips of young girls. Some of these girls have two, three, and even four young babies in tow, each one smaller than the next, like Russian nesting dolls; the baby girls with beads in their hair each one unique as a Tiffany Lamp. Little brown goslings trampling all in a row with their mother goose at the helm, cursing up a blue streak on a cell phone at some unseen boy-father who is not there to defend himself. The children remind her of his failures and wrongdoings, and variations on the word "fuck" are her favorite insults to scream at him on the 79 bus as the children look on, drinking in every obscene word. No one can just skip adolescence. You have to go through it even if, through your own lasciviousness, you find yourself in the position of being a parent.

The girl on the 79 has children crawling all over her. She cannot be more than seventeen and although they're vying for her attention, she refuses to put down her cell phone. Her ability to ignore them is almost trancelike as she giggles like a schoolgirl, texting and social media-ing and leaving them to their own devices to run around the bus like wild moles.

They're screeching, and not even the sound of the music in my headphones can drown them out. The only communication she has with them is to curse, admonishing them for behavior that she will never properly correct. She is weary of them. She hates them. You can see it in her face. As the bus rumbles down a road filled with potholes, her children are unsecured, free to bounce around like gumballs and come back bloody. She cannot be bothered. When I catch her eye, I take the opportunity to shoot her a scornful look, which she roundly ignores to go back to her cell phone. And in that moment, it all becomes clear. She was also raised by a child.

The news that sex causes children has not yet reached the ghetto. The housing projects near my home are positively swarming with children. They run around loose and hang out on the streets until after dark. I see adolescent boys and girls left on their own to claw at each other's genitals, clinging to one another on the bus with more passion that I've seen in adults. The boys roam the streets like hungry lions in search of prey, and I see girls of a tender age dressing far more seductively than should ever be permitted, all while their parents are busy down the street fighting over unfaithful boyfriends and frozen chickens. The carnality goes unchecked and always ends with swollen bellies and dead-end futures.

The girl on the bus is joined by a friend who also has children in tow. They talk about boys. They talk about how they'd like to "get with" this one or that one, and they talk about famous ones, and they talk about the ones who have the nicest asses, the biggest dicks. Grown woman talk out of the mouths of girls. There are few things more powerful than adolescent lasciviousness. The boys talk dirty and in harsh words about things about which they hardly know. Unkind and sexist. All the working parts with none of the knowledge or common sense, and neither will ever be passed to them until it's too late, until they're five babies in and hopeless. The girls giggle and talk about nonsense, and one of their children plops himself in the seat next to me because he can. He is sticky with sugar. I smile at him, and his mother calls him back to her angrily and shoots me another dirty look. He is her reward for being an adult. There is not much teaching to be done when you are seventeen and your mother is thirty-five, so I am not annoyed by this. Their morass will deepen, and the pattern of sex and children will continue. Sex, that adult feeling in the hands of children. They don't know the ways of the world, and now they're thrust into it whether they like it or not. They will begin to resent the children more as they get older for stealing their youth and their opportunities. And money; that is something that will never come, but will still be slightly less elusive than escape.

# Greed

"But those who desire to be rich fall into temptation, into a snare, into many senseless and harmful desires that plunge people into ruin and destruction." (Timothy 6:9)

I am standing beneath the bones of industry. All around me are workmen in fluorescent yellow vests and hard hats shouting instructions at each other as they erect beams and walls, and heavy equipment roars and jackhammers. The autumn sky is littered with progress, and I'm standing underneath it all, noticing for the first time that everything around here is changing. I notice for the first time that the bodega where I bought my cigarettes from the shady Indian people is gone and the nuisance bar just up the street with the shady Black people is gone and the people all around me have started to change complexion. They are working on East Liberty just above my head; changing it just outside my field of vision. The club that used to play hip-hop music is gone, and the whole block has been spruced up with gourmet pizza shops and artisanal cocktail bars. The projects that used to be here are torn down and replaced by a shiny red and white shopping mecca, and there are white people participating in a spin class in the building that used to house the shady Arabic bodega. I just stand there soaking it all in, as if it suddenly just sprung up around me, when a woman approaches and stands beside me. She says, as if we were just in the middle of a conversation,

"You know, they gonna move us all outta here, right?"

East Liberty, the neighborhood just down the street from the East Hills, is changing from the ghetto it once was. It's changing faster than I can keep up. It's changing just like Lawrenceville did before it, and the people who live in my neighborhood have definitely noticed.

"They are going to move us out of here as soon as they need the space," she continues to no one in particular. "Further out until they can't see us."

I stand there with this darkly Black skinned woman that I've never seen before in my life, and we watch the transformation happening right before our eyes. I don't live here, but I don't tell her that. She's looking up at the construction of a newer, shinier place and making plans. I can see it in her eyes. She's wondering where she's going to go, and although I don't want to believe her, I know that she's right. She is the kind of old, diminutive Black woman who is always right. She is someone who's seen this a thousand times before. I pretend to not know what she's talking about, and we both just stare up silent at the harbingers of her imminent dismissal. We stand close enough to be lovers as her scarf flaps in the breeze, and after I've steeped in enough of her reality, I just turn on my heel and walk away, leaving her standing there looking up and wondering what on earth she's going to do.

No one can prosper without taking something, and no one can prosper lavishly without taking lavishly. The word on the street in the East Hills is that "the White People Are Coming." It's just a matter of time. I've seen them with my own eyes. I've seen them in the morning in casual slacks and shirts, surveying the neighborhood and measuring things. It's just a matter of time. It's never done in an obnoxious way. It's always under the guise of progress. It's done very subtly, and those who live here know that we're on borrowed time. There are many things that poverty produces, but noble behavior is not one of them. It frustrates to the point of meanness and strains relationships to the breaking point. It causes inebriation to feel like a daily necessity and makes you hate your neighbor. But this neighborhood is what we've got, and we can't seem to find enough in common with one another to make it better. The only thing that we do have in common is greed. Greed is why we live up here, and that does not escape our attention. The greed, however, is not our own. It is the greed of those who decide that they need more space, more gourmet coffee, and more spin classes. The stories of noble, robust, and hardworking poor people are cherry-picked to make the rest of us feel worthless. These stories are romanticized versions of what poor actually looks like in America. Poverty and racism leave you feeling like less and cause you to behave like less out in the streets. It skews the priorities and, on some days, makes you so angry that you become confused as to where to aim it.

There is an angry hum over the East Hills neighborhood at night under flickering streetlamps when everything appears to be quiet. You can feel it. It causes random children to attack buses and early morning frozen chicken larceny. The anger is misdirected. We all know why we're here. It's because of someone else's greed. The greed of those whose toilets we scrub and security we guard for the promise of a better tomorrow that doesn't come. Someone has to do it and it may as well be us. Often, the quiet around here is split wide open by the sound of a gunshot. The relationship between the haves and the have-nots is anything but symbiotic, and the anger around these parts is electric and alive, and it has to go somewhere. So, we aim it at each other and we rarely ever miss.

# Wrath

"Refrain from anger and turn from wrath; do not fret—it leads only to evil. For evil men will be cut off, but those who hope in the LORD will inherit the land." (Psalm 37:11)

The couch in my apartment is too close to the window. I'm thinking this while bathed in red and blue lights that always seem to turn my small dwelling into a perverted disco. I think that I don't want to be sitting here one day and catch a stray bullet while I'm watching something ridiculous on television. I giggle to myself as the lights dance around the room and I'm moving the couch thinking that the police would find me, bullet to the brain, mouth open in a frozen laugh as reruns of the old *Mary Tyler Moore Show* still crank out canned laughter from my television set. I move the couch because it just makes good sense to move the couch. I move the couch because wrath roams the neighborhood freely; less visible in the daytime but still fully present. When liquor and anger start to flow, so does blood down the sidewalk. I try not to watch the news. I don't really need to because I can hear it all on the 79 the next day. So, I move the couch, knowing full well that Mary Richards and the whole of the WJM-TV news team would never have to move their couches for such a reason. I laugh out loud again, trying to picture Mary Tyler Moore's charming little apartment if it were plopped down in the ghetto. It's unfathomable. The next day, while running out to catch the 79, I stub my toe on the moved couch, and when I board the vehicle, I limp to a seat.

The women sitting behind me didn't know her, but they knew of her. The woman who was murdered yesterday. They are speaking about her casually and not in the shushed tones that one might expect propriety dictates when talking about someone who was just murdered. They knew that he was no good; the one who killed her. He is only twenty years old and she was twenty-eight. She should have known better, they say. I put my headphones on and pretend not to listen, but I am listening intently to their judgment of the situation. They wonder aloud what her children are going to do. She had six of them, and she should have been more focused on them than she was on a twenty-year-old man, they assess. And, as they speak of the dead in less than glowing terms, my whole body becomes heavy with the weight of it all. Six children left motherless. And I have more than likely looked down upon this now dead woman on the 79 several times. I have probably watched her struggling with baby carriage, baby bottles, and diaper bags and decided that her poor decisions have landed her here. But I didn't want her to die.

The women behind me gossip on. Apparently, they argued about money, this murdered woman and her boyfriend. The lack of it, most likely, and then they drank until 2:00 a.m. They fought and then he killed her. And now I can fully picture the ghosts of the youth of her children sitting in the seat across from mine, staring at me with eyes that ask me what I'm going to do beside sit here on the 79 looking down my nose at people every day. I have no answer for them other than I will move the couch. I move away from the window every time I see the lights conditioned like a Pavlovian dog. I wait for the news crews to go away every time someone is killed in the East Hills, and then I emerge from my apartment like Punxsutawney Phil to cast judgment. There is murder and violence ever present around the Eye of Horus. It is the hum of anger that transforms itself to wrath that generates dead Black bodies around here. Men, women, and children murdered by their own on a shockingly regular basis. It's not just a news story when you live in the middle of it. It not just something to cluck your tongue at.

The women behind me judge on. They shift their own babies from knee to knee with the rocking of the 79, and they gossip. I don't want to hear them anymore. I turn on my music. It's the theme from *The Mary Tyler Moore Show*.

I once heard someone on the 79 say that if everyone did the right thing all the time, there would be no one left to work for nothing. People from other neighborhoods look at us up here and assume that we are what's leftover and, on some level, we deserve to be here. Our bad decisions are what have led us to this place. But if everyone made the right decisions all the time, there would be no one for everyone to look down on, and it is in this way that capitalism works. We live here so that others can convince themselves that the worst of human instincts does not dwell in their neighborhoods. Only here. They can convince themselves that no lover's quarrel has ever ended in ridiculous behavior. They can convince themselves that no white child has ever done vandalism, and they can convince themselves that "something like that" would never happen where they live. They can convince themselves that there has never been a drunk in their neighborhood who was in dire need of mental health care. We are zoo-ed, and the chances of getting out are slim to none. They wonder aloud why society can't cast a play in hell and get angels for actors. They feature our awful behavior live every night on your local news before the blood on the sidewalks even dries. But we're still here.

There was a time, long before my arrival, when the enormous, pockmarked parking lot across the street from my apartment was a shopping center. Now it is home to a single megachurch where people worship a Jesus who is never going to come for them. The only ones who are coming are the police who cruise the streets slowly day and night like sentinels.

Sometimes I wake up early in the morning with the sun and I find myself missing Jody. One night, the blue lights came, but this time they were cut through with red ones, and I heard a lot of men talking outside, and then they drove away in an ambulance and I haven't seen Jody since. New people moved in and told me that he died. He finally got out. It is at this time of the early morning that I know that I will not sleep. So I go outside to stare out at the parking lot and wait for the sun long before the neighborhood wakes to put its two cents in and tell me who I am. I already know who I am, and I'm not fooling anyone. I am not special. I am every bit a part of this neighborhood as those I complain about and like to pretend that I'm better than. I stare out at the empty megachurch parking lot with the sun coming up all around me, and I try to imagine what it must have been like a long time ago bustling with activity and commerce. But I can't really picture it.

I will be sitting on my hands and moving away from the window on cue when the red and blue lights burst through until they come to take the East Hills. And they will come and take it when they need more room. This I believe is certain. We will never ban together to stop it, and I'm just as guilty of inaction as anyone else up here in this ghetto. We hate each other up here. I'm not going anywhere. None of us are. Until the white people come to take it all away, this is all our powerlessness tells us that we can do until we are moved again, and I will move right along with everyone else. And while I stand there feeling the sun's first morning warmth on my back, I can hear the 79 beginning its first circle of the morning at the caruncle of the Eye of Horus, where it will go around and around and around all the livelong day.

*"79" was originally published in* Creative Nonfiction.

# Acknowledgments

This book has been a communal effort, produced by many people who have created, sustained, supported, and participated in the strange and wonderful project that is Belt Publishing, from its founding in 2014 until today. It has been a gift and honor to be part of this community.

The person most responsible for this book is Phoebe Mogharei, who understood the assignment in the most profound way. Michael Jauchen worked alongside her, on this and on many of the books whose essays are included here. David Wilson, whose covers have created the look, mission, and feel of the press, designed this one, too. Anna Clark, editor of the first "real" book from this press, took great time and care crafting the introduction. I am continually inspired by her.

This "best of" compilation would not exist without the editors of the many City Anthologies whose essays are included here. To Martha Bayne, Eric Boyd, Ben Gwin, Justin Kern, Samuel Love, Jacqueline Marino, Zach Mortice, Nick Swartsell, Richey Piiparinen, Ryan Schuessler, Terrion L. Williamson, and Kevin Whiteneir, Jr.: your dedication to editing offered not just an opportunity to the best writers of your city but also a gift to the readers of that city, not to mention anyone with an interest in the complicated, fascinating, and wonderful life of that city, and a particular place during a particular time. To the writers who are included here, it goes without saying (but I am saying it anyway): this book was written by you, and it is to you that the credit goes.

Finally, I would like to shout out the city of Cleveland and the Clevelanders who helped Belt Publishing come into being, nourished and grounded what would have otherwise been just a floundering idea dreamt up in the basement of the Happy Dog, around a table while drinking beers—an idea made material by the writers and independent booksellers in town.

No one was more important to dreaming Belt into being than Peter Debelak, to whom, as he would say, I am grateful. Boy, do I wish I could give him a copy of this book. He is sorely missed.

# Contributors

**Michael R. Allen** serves as executive director of the National Building Arts Center, a museum of the American built environment, as well as senior lecturer in architecture, landscape architecture, and urban design at the Sam Fox School of Design and Visual Arts at Washington University in St. Louis. Allen's scholarly and critical articles have appeared in a wide range of scholarly and popular sources, such as *Buildings and Landscapes*, *CityLab*, *Disegno*, *Forty-Five Journal*, *Hyperallergic*, *Next City*, *PLATFORM*, *Temporary Art Review*, the *St. Louis American*, the *St. Louis Post-Dispatch*, and *Studies in the History of Gardens and Designed Landscapes*. He is one of the convenors of Housing Blocs, a global research project on mass housing examining links between the United States of America and postsocialist Europe.

**Gint Aras** has been trapped on planet earth since 1973. He's an award-winning and anthologized author whose works include the novels *Finding the Moon in Sugar* (Infinity, 2009) and *The Fugue (Tortoise, 2016)*, and the memoir *Relief by Execution: A Visit to Mauthausen (Little Bound Books, 2020)*. His short prose and translations have appeared in over a dozen journals, including *Quarterly West*, *Antique Children*, *LitReactor*, *Hypertext*, and the *St. Petersburg Review*. A textbook titled *What Is a College Student?* (Kendall-Hunt, 2023) is his most recent publication. He lives in Oak Park, Illinois, with his family.

**Sophia Benoit** is the author of the book *Well, This Is Exhausting*. She has regular columns in *GQ* and *Bustle* and has written for *WSJ*, the *Guardian*, the *Cut*, *Fatherly*, *Insider*, *Refinery29*, *Allure*, and more. Sophia does not have an MFA from anywhere and probably isn't going back to grad school, much to the chagrin of her father. She lives in LA with her boyfriend and her dog, Party.

**Sharon Bloyd-Peshkin** is a professor of Journalism at Columbia College Chicago, where she is the Faculty Fellow for Civic Engagement, and an accredited Solutions Journalism trainer.

**Brian Broome**'s debut memoir, *Punch Me Up to the Gods*, is an NYT Editor's Pick and the winner of the 2021 Kirkus Prize for Nonfiction. He is a contributing columnist at the *Washington Post*. His work has also appeared in *Hippocampus, Poets and Writers, Medium*, and more. Brian was a K. Leroy Irvis Fellow and an instructor in the Writing Program at the University of Pittsburgh. He has been a finalist in the Moth storytelling competition and won the grand prize in Carnegie Mellon University's Martin Luther King Writing Awards. Brian also won a VANN Award from the Pittsburgh Black Media Federation for journalism in 2019. His film, *Garbage*, won the Audience Choice Award at the Cortada Short Film Festival and was a semifinalist in the Portland Short Fest.

**Phil Christman** is a writer, a lecturer at the University of Michigan, and the editor of the *Michigan Review of Prisoner Creative Writing*.

**Anna Clark** is a writer in Detroit and an investigative journalist for ProPublica. She's the author *The Poisoned City: Flint's Water and the American Urban Tragedy*, which won the Hillman Prize for Book Journalism and the Rachel Carson environmental book award. Anna also edited *A Detroit Anthology*, a Michigan Notable Book, and wrote a short book of literary history. Her writing has appeared in the *New York Times*, the *Washington Post*, the *New Republic, Elle*, the *Guardian, Next City* and *Belt Magazine*, among other publications. Anna was a Fulbright fellow in creative writing in Kenya and a Knight-Wallace journalism fellow at the University of Michigan. She teaches nonfiction in Alma College's MFA program in creative writing.

**Harmony Cox** is one of the managing editors of the popular satire website the Belladonna. She hosts Story Club Columbus, frequently performs at local literary events, and her work has appeared in *Narratively, McSweeney's*, and elsewhere.

**Lyndsey Ellis** is a writer, teaching artist and community organizer who is passionate about exploring regional history and intergenerational experiences in the Midwest. Her work appears in *Kweli Journal, Narratively, Shondaland*, Catapult, the *Rumpus, Literary Hub, Electric Literature* and several anthologies. Ellis has been a recipient of the Friends of American Writers Literature Award, San Francisco Foundation's Joseph Henry

Jackson Literary Award, Barbara Deming Memorial Fund, Washington University's Inaugural Heartland Journalism Fellowship, and an artist support grant from the Regional Arts Commission St. Louis, which helped her launch a local intergenerational storytelling workshop series. Her debut novel, *Bone Broth*, was published by Hidden Timber Books in 2021 and was a first-year read at Maryville University in St. Louis for two consecutive years.

**Aaron Foley** is a journalist and writer living between Brooklyn and Detroit. He is the author of fiction and nonfiction, including *Boys Come First* and *How to Live in Detroit Without Being a Jackass*. His work has also appeared in *This American Life*, the *PBS NewsHour*, *Jalopnik*, CNN and more.

**Tanisha C. Ford** is an award-winning writer, cultural critic, and professor of history at the Graduate Center, CUNY. She is the author of *Dressed in Dreams: A Black Girl's Love Letter to the Power of Fashion*; *Kwame Brathwaite: Black Is Beautiful*; and *Liberated Threads: Black Women, Style, and the Global Politics of Soul*.

**LaToya Ruby Frazier** was born in 1982 in Braddock, Pennsylvania. Her artistic practice spans a range of media, including photography, video, performance, installation art, and books, and centers on the nexus of social justice, cultural change, and commentary on the American experience. In various interconnected bodies of work, Frazier uses collaborative storytelling with the people who appear in her artwork to address topics of industrialism, Rust Belt revitalization, environmental justice, access to health care, access to clean water, workers' rights, human rights, family, and communal history. Frazier's work has been the subject of numerous solo exhibitions at institutions in the US and Europe, including the Brooklyn Museum of Art; Seattle Art Museum; the Institute of Contemporary Art in Boston; Contemporary Art Museum, Houston; Musée des Arts Contemporains, Grand-Hornu, Belgium; CAPC Musée d'Art Contemporain de Bordeaux, France; and more.

**Ken Germanson**, president emeritus of the Wisconsin Labor History Society, is recognized as a knowledgeable historian on workers and the labor movement in Wisconsin. A onetime newspaper reporter and editor, Germanson worked as a union representative and top official of the former International Union, Allied Industrial Workers Union (now United

Steelworkers) for nearly thirty years. He was president of the Labor History Society for seventeen years and continues as a volunteer for the society. After his retirement from his union work in 1992, Germanson was employed for twenty-four years for Community Advocates in Milwaukee, working on behalf of low-income families in the areas of child abuse prevention, gun violence strategies, and health care access. In 2018, Germanson was awarded the honorary doctor of humane letters by the University of Wisconsin–Milwaukee for his work in the community and for preserving and promoting the history of labor in Wisconsin. In 2014, the City of Milwaukee Common Council awarded Germanson the Frank P. Zeidler Community Service Award.

**Vivian Gibson** was raised on Bernard Street in Mill Creek Valley and has lived in New York City and Liberia, West Africa. After retiring at sixty-six, she started writing short stories about her childhood memories in a segregated St. Louis community. The Missouri Humanities Council honored her with a Literary Achievement Award in 2020. The Missouri Library Association named her 2022 Author of the Year, and the Library of Congress recognized Vivian Gibson's *The Last Children of Mill Creek* to represent the state of Missouri's literary heritage at the 2023 National Book Festival in Washington, DC.

**Ben Gwin** is the author of the novel, *Clean Time*, and the book, *Team Building: A Memoir about Family and the Fight for Workers' Rights*. He was also the editor of the anthology *The Pittsburgh Neighborhood Guidebook*. Ben's fiction and essays have appeared in the *Rumpus*, *Normal School*, *Lit Hub*, and others. He lives in Pittsburgh with his child.

**Britt Julious** is a writer, editor, essayist, and storyteller focusing on subjects that intersect the worlds of art, culture, race, feminism, and politics. A firm believer in the underground, the avant-garde, and the underdog, Britt currently serves as the music critic for the *Chicago Tribune*. As a freelance journalist, she has written for *Pitchfork*, *Harper's Bazaar*, *Glamour*, the *Cut*, the *New York Times*, and many others. In 2023, Britt was an inaugural fellow of the University of Chicago's Critic's Table. She is also a recipient of the Studs Terkel award in journalism for her work spotlighting underserved communities. She is currently working on a book project and a podcast.

**Sarah Kendzior** is a writer who lives in St. Louis, Missouri. She is the bestselling author of *The View from Flyover Country*, *Hiding in Plain Sight*, and *They Knew*. Her next book, *The Last American Road Trip*, will be published in 2025. Kendzior has a PhD in anthropology and writes about politics, history, and travel at sarahkendzior.substack.com.

**Jacqueline Marino**'s work has appeared in the *Washington Post*, *Belt*, and the literary journal *River Teeth*, among other publications. In recent years, she's reported on rural health and the Mahoning River for Ideastream Public Media—and won Edward R. Murrow Awards for her coverage. She is a former associate editor of *Cleveland Magazine* and the author of the book *White Coats: Three Journeys through an American Medical School* (Kent State University Press, 2012), the winner of a 2013 Independent Publisher Book Award (Silver, Education). Her edited book, *Car Bombs to Cookie Tables: The Youngstown Anthology* (Belt Publishing, 2015, 2nd edition, 2020), amplifies the voices of writers from her hometown of Youngstown, Ohio, which captivated Bruce Springsteen and continues to enthrall national journalists and filmmakers, especially during election years.

**Annie Maroon** is a writer from western Pennsylvania. She previously worked as a reporter for *MassLive* and is now a freelance writer and photographer in the Boston area. Her work is online at anniemaroon.com.

**Dani McClain** reports on race, parenting, and reproductive health. McClain's writing has appeared in outlets including the *New York Times*, *Time*, the *Atlantic*, *Harper's Bazaar* and *Colorlines*. Her work has been recognized by the National Lesbian and Gay Journalists Association, the National Association of Black Journalists, Planned Parenthood Federation of America, and she's received a James Aronson Award for Social Justice Journalism. McClain is a contributing writer at the *Nation*. She was a staff reporter at the *Milwaukee Journal Sentinel* and has worked as a strategist with organizations including Color of Change and Drug Policy Alliance. Her book, *We Live for the We: The Political Power of Black Motherhood*, was published in 2019 by Bold Type Books and was shortlisted in 2020 for a Hurston/Wright Legacy Award. She was the Cincinnati public library's writer-in-residence in 2020 and 2021. Learn more about her work here: https://linktr.ee/dani_mcclain

**Mark Oliver** is a Canadian writer who spent most of his life in an Amish community.

**Joseph S. Pete**'s great-grandfather fled Macedonia to avoid conscription in the Ottoman Empire in World War I. After arriving at Ellis Island, he learned about the opportunity of steelworker jobs in Gary, Indiana, where he sipped wine, listened to classical music, and walked to work at US Steel's Gary Works mill every day. His son Stanley led the union at American Bridge in Gary, where he helped build American icons like the Sears Tower, the John Hancock Center, the St. Louis Arch, and the Houston Astrodome. Stanley's grandson Joseph now covers Gary for the *Times of Northwest Indiana*, and often volunteers in the Steel City. His newspaper articles hang on many walls in Gary, especially in the Miller neighborhood.

**Audrey Petty**'s first home neighborhood in Chicago was Chatham. She is the editor of *High Rise Stories: Voices from Chicago Public Housing* (Voice of Witness/Haymarket Press) and coeditor of *The Long Term: Resisting Life Sentences, Working Toward Freedom* (Haymarket Press). Her writing has appeared in such publications as *Saveur, Oxford American, Poetry, Callaloo, Gravy,* the *Southern Review, Columbia Journal,* and the *Best Food Writing* anthology.

**Erik Piepenburg** is a regular contributor to the *New York Times*, where he writes about LGBTQ issues, horror movies, and pop culture. His book about the history of gay restaurants is to be published by Hachette in 2025. Originally from Cleveland, he lives in New York City.

**Nartana Premachandra** is story editor for the international NY-based journal *Parabola, the Search for Meaning*. She is also a classical Indian dancer and president of dances of India in St. Louis, Missouri. Dances of India, a 2023 National Endowment for the Arts Award recipient, is now in its forty-seventh season and is one of the oldest classical Indian dance companies in the US. Please visit her at NartanaPremachandra.com

**Kathleen Rooney** is a founding editor of Rose Metal Press, a nonprofit publisher of literary work in hybrid genres, as well as a founding member of Poems While You Wait, a team of poets and their typewriters who compose commissioned poetry on demand. She teaches in the English Department at DePaul University, and her recent books include the national bestseller *Lillian Boxfish Takes a Walk* (St. Martin's Press 2017) and the novel *Cher Ami and Major Whittlesey* (Penguin 2020). *Where Are the Snows*, her latest poetry collection, was chosen by Kazim Ali for the X. J. Kennedy Prize and published by Texas Review Press in Fall 2022. She lives in Chicago with her spouse, the writer Martin Seay.

**Tara Rose** is a Michigan-raised freelance writer who now lives in Winston-Salem, North Carolina. She writes personal essays and memoirs about class struggle, pop culture, mental health, and the human condition.

**Samantha Sanders** is a Brooklyn-based writer/editor and visual artist originally from Cincinnati, Ohio. She's previously worked for *Writer's Digest* and *Artists Magazine* and her work has appeared online at the Awl, Catapult, and Popula.

**Ryan Scavnicky** (Scav) is a storyteller creating architectural discourse through experimental media. Using memes, TikToks, op-eds, group chats, Twitch broadcasts, Discord servers, and traditional print media, Scav challenges the status quo of what is accepted as bona fide disciplinary content. He studied at L'Ecole Speciale d'Architecture in Paris, DAAP in Cincinnati, and SCI-Arc in Los Angeles. Professionally, he has worked as a designer at various scales of architectural production on three different continents. Scav is currently an assistant professor of practice at Marywood University, where he is pioneering the launch of the Bachelors of Virtual Architecture program.

**Connie Schultz** is a Pulitzer Prize–winning writer, a nationally syndicated columnist with Creators Syndicate, and Professional in Residence in the journalism school at Kent State University, her alma mater. She is the author of *Life Happens, . . . And His Lovely Wife*, *The Daughters of Erietown*, and *Lola and the Troll*. Schultz lives in Cleveland with her husband, Sherrod Brown, and their two rescue dogs, Franklin and Walter. They have four children and seven grandchildren.

**Megan Stielstra** is the author of three collections: *Everyone Remain Calm*, *Once I Was Cool*, and *The Wrong Way to Save Your Life*. Her work appears in the *Best American Essays*, *New York Times*, the *Believer*, *Poets & Writers*, *Tin House*, and elsewhere. A longtime company member with 2nd Story, she has told stories for National Public Radio, the Museum of Contemporary Art, and regularly with the Paper Machete live news magazine at the Green Mill. She teaches creative nonfiction at Northwestern University and is an editor with Northwestern University Press.

**Anne Trubek** is the founder and publisher of Belt Publishing. She is the author of *So You Want To Publish A Book?* (Belt Publishing, 2020), and editor of *Voices from the Rust Belt* (Picador, 2018). She is also author of *The History and Uncertain Future of Handwriting* (Bloomsbury, 2016) and *A Skeptic's Guide to Writers' Houses* (University of Pennsylvania Press, 2010). She has been publishing her Notes from a Small Press newsletter since 2018.

**Kim-Marie Walker** is a nonfiction and fiction writer recently published in *Literary Hub, Killens Review of Arts and Letters, Our Voices, Our Stories Anthology, Birds Thumb, The Compassion Anthology, Talking Stick, Track Four, NILVX*; and author of *Zebras from Heaven*, a memoir. A travel memoir about her solo pilgrimage to America's transatlantic slave trade ports, honoring the first footsteps of Middle Passage Africans, is a work in progress. Writing residencies include VONA/Voices Writers Workshop, Rhode Island Writers Colony, and Wildacres Retreat. For more information, please visit www.kimmariewalker.com.

**David Weathersby** is a filmmaker/videographer and the founder of City Vanguard, an arts organization that helps independent filmmakers create community-based documentaries for educational and cultural institutions. As a director, he has produced films, documentaries, music videos, and video art projects. His past projects include the documentaries *The Color of Art, It's Different in Chicago, Sapphire and Crystals, Thee Debauchery Ball, and Kinky and Loving It*. His work has been featured on The Africa Channel, WTTW, and various film festivals including Pan African Film Festival, San Diego Black Film Festival, Roxbury International Film Festival, Chicago Onscreen, Chicago South Side Film Festival, Collected Voices Film Festival, Black Harvest Film Festival, Image Union Film Festival, and The Chicago Short Comedy Film Festival. In 2018, he was awarded a Black Excellence award for best director by the African American Arts Alliance of Chicago.